We recently lost our beloved pet "Bear," who was not
only our best and dearest friend but also the "Vice President of
Sunshine" here at Atlantic Publishing. He did not receive a salary
but worked tirelessly 24 hours a day to please his parents. Bear
was a rescue dog that turned around and showered myself, my wife
Sherri, his grandparents Jean, Bob and Nancy and every person and
animal he met (maybe not rabbits) with friendship and love. He
made a lot of people smile every day.

We wanted you to know that a portion of the profits of this book
will be donated to The Humane Society of
the United States.

–Douglas & Sherri Brown

THE HUMANE SOCIETY
OF THE UNITED STATES ©

The human-animal bond is as old as human history. We cherish our animal companions for their unconditional affection and acceptance. We feel a thrill when we glimpse wild creatures in their natural habitat or in our own backyard.

Unfortunately, the human-animal bond has at times been weakened. Humans have exploited some animal species to the point of extinction.

The Humane Society of the United States makes a difference in the lives of animals here at home and worldwide. The HSUS is dedicated to creating a world where our relationship with animals is guided by compassion. We seek a truly humane society in which animals are respected for their intrinsic value, and where the human-animal bond is strong.

Want to help animals? We have plenty of suggestions. Adopt a pet from a local shelter, join The Humane Society and be a part of our work to help companion animals and wildlife. You will be funding our educational, legislative, investigative and outreach projects in the U.S. and across the globe.

Or perhaps you'd like to make a memorial donation in honor of a pet, friend or relative? You can through our Kindred Spirits program. And if you'd like to contribute in a more structured way, our Planned Giving Office has suggestions about estate planning, annuities, and even gifts of stock that avoid capital gains taxes.

Maybe you have land that you would like to preserve as a lasting habitat for wildlife. Our Wildlife Land Trust can help you. Perhaps the land you want to share is a backyard—that's enough. Our Urban Wildlife Sanctuary Program will show you how to create a habitat for your wild neighbors.

So you see, it's easy to help animals. And The HSUS is here to help.

The Humane Society of the United States
2100 L Street NW
Washington, DC 20037
202-452-1100
www.hsus.org

Table of Contents

Foreword

Ostriches and people who have debt that they cannot afford often are very similar in that both tend to hide their heads in the sand and hope the world will pass them by. Bankruptcy is a very serious legal matter and, if you are considering filing for bankruptcy, the more informed you are the better off you will be. Hiding your head in the sand and ignoring your financial problems is not a successful or rational method for dealing with debt.

If you are now considering bankruptcy, you probably have had a major "life event" occur. This life event may have been a loss of income, job loss, divorce, business failure, or maybe you just became overextended and now are overwhelmed. This book will help you examine what you should know about the bankruptcy process and how it can give you the fresh start that you want and need to move forward with your life.

Matt Pelc, in *What to Do When You Have to File Bankruptcy*, has provided an interesting and insightful analysis of the issues facing the average person when they are considering bankruptcy. As a shareholder and the managing director of the bankruptcy department in one of Michigan's most experienced law firms, I found the information contained in this book to be both relevant and helpful. Not only will it provide consumers with a complete analysis of what to be concerned with when filing for bankruptcy, but it offers an excellent nuts and bolts review of bankruptcy issues that face a practitioner and his or her support staff. In fact, I have made Matt's book required reading for all of my support staff.

When I began practicing bankruptcy law over 17 years ago, there were not opportunities to learn the practice from books and manuals, an attorney would have pick it up over time. This book changes much of that. Pelc's book brings the consumer into the world of bankruptcy and provides them with the knowledge that it takes most practitioners many years to obtain. The book does not replace the need to have an attorney, but it assists in educating and informing consumers so that they are better able to choose a knowledgeable attorney to help them. If they do seek to file bankruptcy without an attorney, *What to Do When You Have to File Bankruptcy* provides an excellent fundamental analysis of bankruptcy law in a way that anyone can clearly understand it.

Brian Joel Small

Shareholder

Thav, Gross, Steinway & Bennett, P.C.

30150 Telegraph Road, Suite 444

Bingham Farms, MI 48025

248-645-1700

http://www.StopCreditorCalls.com

http://www.Thavgross.com

E-mail: bankruptcy@thavgross.com

Brian Joel Small is a Shareholder in the law firm of Thav, Gross, Steinway & Bennett, P.C. He has been practicing bankruptcy law since 1992. His practice includes bankruptcy and corporate dissolution. He attended the University of Michigan for his undergraduate studies and law school at the T.C. Williams School of Law at the University of Richmond. He was admitted to the State Bar of Michigan in 1992. He is a member of the National Association of Consumer Bankruptcy Attorneys (NACBA), the American Bankruptcy Institute (ABI), and the National Association of Chapter Thirteen Trustees (NACTT). He is a board member of the Consumer Bankruptcy Association in Michigan and its current Vice-President. He practices before all Judges in the Eastern and Western Districts of Michigan and he is admitted before the United States Court of Appeals for the Sixth Circuit. Small often speaks at Local and National Bankruptcy Seminars and is currently co-authoring a practice manual for attorneys in the area of bankruptcy.

Introduction

"Bankruptcy."

To many, that is a dirty word.

To some, it means the end of the board game Monopoly, when one person loses all their money, and it is signified by a drawing of the game's iconic mascot, with his pockets turned inside out, looking forlorn.

What comes to your mind when you hear the word "bankruptcy?"

For those fortunate individuals who have never faced financial dire straight, the word bankruptcy may have a negative connotation to it. You may think it is people bucking the system, living way over their means, spending irresponsibly, or just trying to take the easy way out of a tough situation.

For the unfortunate who are struggling with their monetary situation and are tired of being harassed by phone, mail, and wage garnishments, bankruptcy may seem like the perfect way to make their troubles go away forever. They hope to wash away every debt they have with no more money coming out of their pockets.

The truth lies somewhere in the middle.

To declare bankruptcy does not mean a person has no income source and is now utterly penniless. Most people are still employed or are receiving unemployment benefits, child support, family contributions, or other sources that provide an income flow into the household, but that income flow may not be enough to pay all the person's debts and the late fees that continue to mount.

People file bankruptcy for a variety of reasons:

- Sudden loss of a job

- IRS lien

- Hospital bills

- To stop a repossession of a vehicle or a foreclosure on a home

- Large property tax increases or large mortgage payment increases stemming from an adjustable rate mortgage

- Divorce

- Any other unforeseeable event

Depending on which type of bankruptcy (known as a Chapter) you are eligible to file, you may have to pay back either a portion of or your entire debt, but you will be under the protection of a branch of the United States government, which will stop your creditors from harassing you. Also, some debts, such as unpaid taxes, child support, and student loans, may survive the conclusion of the bankruptcy, and you will be required to continue to pay these obligations. We will address these issues later.

Many people feel shame or embarrassment when filing bankruptcy, but know that you are not alone in this process.

The chart below, compiled and displayed on the United States Courts government Web site (**http://www.uscourts. gov**), shows that while the numbers of bankruptcy filings have decreased by 28 percent in the last year, the four years leading up to 2007 showed an incredible amount of filings. The final month of this study, September 2007, showed a marked increase in cases filed. According to the US Court's Web site, it is the most since September 2006.

Business and Non-Business Filings Years Ended September 30, 2003-2007			
Year	Business	Non-Business	Total
2007	25,925	775,344	801,269
2006	27,333	1,085,209	1,112,542
2005	34,222	1,748,421	1,782,643
2004	34,817	1,584,170	1,618,987
2003	36,183	1,625,813	1,661,996

Even the rich and famous have the occasional stumble and seek the relief and protection that bankruptcy provides. This was not a black mark on these celebrities; to tell you the truth, for many of them, it was quite the contrary. Many of them went onto even greater success after they filed.

- P.T. Barnum filed for bankruptcy in 1894. Shortly after filing, his famous circus was born.

- Milton Hershey failed at four candy companies prior to his fifth and extremely successful company, which is now called the Hershey Foods Corporation. In each unsuccessful business, Hershey filed for bankruptcy protection.

- Henry Ford ran two unsuccessful companies, one of which went bankrupt. His third company, the Ford Motor Company, was a success.

- Donald Trump was on top of the world until his business declared bankruptcy in 1990. The Apprentice host regained his wealth, even before achieving television stardom.

As you can see, declaring bankruptcy is not the end of the world. There is no question that bankruptcy is a difficult, challenging process with many hurdles. You will interact and discuss your finances with your attorney (if you hire one, which is always highly recommended), the trustee, your creditors, and a judge. The fact that so many people are overseeing your finances and commenting on your financial lifestyle may be frustrating, but if you and your family commit to the process of bankruptcy, you will emerge better on the other end.

This book is divided into three sections and is designed to help you gain an understanding of the bankruptcy process so that you can make informed decisions, from filing to discharge.

In the first section, we will delve into your preparation for filing bankruptcy by covering the following topics:

- A brief look back on how you got into this situation

- Learning to evaluate your finances, determine your monthly income, and decide whether bankruptcy is the right course of action for you at this time

- Alternatives to filing bankruptcy

- Obtaining, effectively reviewing, and contesting any inaccuracies on your credit report

- Listing the types of debts you may have and describing how they will fit in with your bankruptcy

- Describing the similarities and differences between a Chapter 7 and a Chapter 13, and determining which chapter you are eligible to file

- Thc importance of having an attorney and finding the right one

The second section will outline the "guts" of the bankruptcy world:

- Laws

- Recent major changes

- Frequently asked questions

- Bankruptcy myths

- Your timeline and court hearings from filing until discharge

Finally, the last section will provide a brief overview of your post-bankruptcy life and how to rebuild your credit and obtain future car and home loans.

Right now, only you (and those nagging creditors) know your current financial situation. To begin the process of declaring bankruptcy, you need to sit down and evaluate whether bankruptcy is the right option for you at this time.

A quick note about some of the following: We will extensively discuss the need to use the Internet for your research before, during, and after bankruptcy. It is very important that you do so. We know that not everyone who will read this has access to a computer or the Internet, but if that is the case for you, please try to make other arrangements. Seek out a good friend or family member who will let you borrow their services. If that is not a viable option, go to your local community library. If you have not been to one in a long time, libraries are much different than you remember as a kid doing research projects there. Most of them have many computers with Internet access for you to use free of charge, just like the books on the shelf. Sometimes, the Internet is the best or only option of obtaining this material.

So, with that it mind, let us get started.

PART I

BEFORE
FILING

CHAPTER 1

How We Got Here

"Why is there so much month left at the end of the money?"
– John Barrymore, American Actor

If you are even remotely considering bankruptcy, then your financial situation is in bad shape. In most cases, this did not happen overnight. While you should not overly dwell on the past, a brief review of your spending habits may help you out in the future, after your bankruptcy case has been discharged, if you choose that avenue.

Have You Overspent?

Financial troubles can result from many different events.

If you or someone in your household unexpectedly lost their job, someone fell ill, resulting in thousands of dollars worth of medical bills, or a repair was needed inside a home that cost a small fortune, financial troubles did arrive practically overnight.

For others, irresponsible spending has led you down this dark path. Ladies, do you get your hair cut and styled at a beauty salon monthly, which costs $100 or more? Most areas have unisex haircut venues that provide much of the same services that beauty shops offer – for less than half the cost. Guys, is it necessary to subscribe to every sports cable package?

These are luxuries, and for some, it is hard to live without luxuries, but when it is hard to make ends meet at the end of the month, it is more prudent that these take a backseat to the mortgage, utilities, food, and gas.

Perhaps at the grocery store, you pass up every store brand in favor of the brand named varieties. The store brands are not an inferior product, they just cut out the middle man. Instead of being manufactured by a large company, then shipped to the grocer's warehouse, and then shipped to the store, store brands are often manufactured in or near the grocery warehouse and then shipped to the store. This process involves one less step, and the savings from that one less step are passed on to the consumer. Brand names on average run about $.50 to $1 more than their store counterparts. This may not seem like much, but when you buy $200-$300 worth of groceries each month, the savings will add up.

When you bought your last car, did you get it loaded with options like a moon roof, satellite radio, leather seats, remote car starter, or other, potentially frivolous luxury items? As as much as you may think you cannot live without them, remember that your parents and earlier generations lived without these "toys" on their vehicles, and so can you.

Are You Too Giving?

Do you regularly give to a charity or contribute weekly at your place of worship? These are noble deeds and you should be commended for thinking of others. Yet, it is time to start thinking about your family. If cutting out the $100 per month to a reliable cause will help you pay a bill or two for the month, then sadly, the charitable donation has got to stop. These donations can be resumed when you are financially stable again. Many churches require members to donate weekly, and some require a percentage of a family's income to be contributed. Perhaps, you can speak with your pastor or clergyman about suspending your donations or reducing them until you are back on your feet again. If you chose to file bankruptcy, you may not necessarily have to stop or reduce your charitable contributions. But if your budget is particularly low, this may become an issue.

There are many more examples of these types of situations. The point of this section was merely to point out that had certain cuts, sacrifices, and clever shopping skills been used, your situation might not be as bleak as it now appears.

We will learn more about being a smart consumer in Part III of this book, where we will focus on your future in a post-bankruptcy world.

But It is Not My Fault

Some of the events that have transpired to bring you toward the brink of bankruptcy are indeed not your fault. These are events that spring up suddenly. It could be an expensive situation that needs to be dealt with immediately, such as damage to a home or vehicle used for employment or transportation to work.

Unemployment

Most economic pundits acknowledge that we are on precipice of a prolonged recession; for some, the recession is here. According to the United States Department of Labor, 5 percent (7.6 million) of Americans were out of work in January 2008.

A particularly hard-hit area is the industrialized north. Leading the nation with a 7.6 percent unemployment rate, Michigan continues to lose jobs due to the ever-shrinking domestic automobile industry. Yet, if you think the hardships end in this state, you are mistaken.

Many other sectors in business and industry also continue to downsize and layoff their workforce. Despite efforts from some congressional members to extend unemployment benefits, the idea was quickly snuffed out. This means most people who lose their jobs have only six months to find a new position in a shaky job market.

Hospital Bills

No one wants to get sick, particularly when they have no insurance or their insurance does not cover certain procedures. Extended hospital stays or recovery time from a major surgery more often than not results in another problem – the inability to work. If your employer does not provide disability, not only are the hospital bills piling up, but so are the household bills because there is no income to pay them. That is a double whammy most people cannot recover from.

Divorce

For many people, divorce can push them into financial distress.

The cost of a divorce can greatly fluctuate with the degree in which the husband and wife agree or disagree on certain aspects of the split-up. Attorney fees are never cheap, and if there is a custody battle, some judges will order psychiatric counseling for the children. Also, if the separation of estate is being contested, some attorneys suggest hiring an appraiser for the proper valuation of the property.

For some, divorce is just too pricey. Many times, a debtor in bankruptcy will state that he or she is separated and will be asked if a divorce is pending by the trustee or judge. Often, the debtor will say that a divorce is not pending, it is just too expensive.

Out of Control Credit Cards

Credit cards prey on the vulnerability of most people. Everyone wants things that they cannot afford. But if they can pay it off over a period of three to five years, then they may go for it.

Credit card companies are billion-dollar corporations with savvy marketing people working for them. They use cutesy, clever, and comical television advertisements, along with some buzz words and phrases, to reel consumers in. Here are some of the most common:

"NO PAYMENTS UNTIL 2010!"

"PRE-APPROVAL"

"APPROVAL GUARANTEED!"

"BRUISED AND BROKEN CREDIT ACCEPTED!"

Maybe in the past, you have applied for and received a credit card, not for a frivolous spending spree, but with the good intention of paying off an old bill. This is laudable, but sadly, this did nothing to help your finances. It may have bought you a few months with no creditors harassing you, but the new credit card company wants its payments too, and is at least as aggressive to get its money.

This is what many in the bankruptcy community refer to as, "Taking from Peter to pay Paul."

Some credit card companies send your interest rate through the stratosphere if you so much as miss one payment. Obtaining credit cards is simply not a good idea for bailing you out of debt.

Rising Housing Costs

"What goes up most come down," is a popular phrase in today's lexicon. Sir Isaac Newton originally said it, but he obviously did not fathom inflation, gas prices, and housing costs.

Electric, natural gas, and water costs continue to rise faster than inflation, and if that is not enough, cities, townships, and counties continue rapidly increasing homeowners' property taxes; add that to the growing problem with adjustable rate mortgages (or ARM loans). Paying equal or less than one would pay for rent in an apartment or condominium is exciting for most people; that is what ARM loans provide. Look out three to four years later, though, when the interest rate and the payment increase. In some cases, the payment increase is so high that it reaches beyond the means of the household income.

Accepting the Past and Looking to the Future

Now that you have looked at your past spending habits and the factors that were beyond your control, it is time to move on. Acknowledge that issues have happened, whether it was in your control or not, and understand that millions of people have these same problems. You are just smart enough to realize that something needs to be done.

So let us move on from the past and look to the future.

CHAPTER 2

Should I File Bankruptcy?

"It is truly said: It does not take much strength to do things, but it requires great strength to decide what to do."
– *Chow Ching, Chinese Writer*

The title of this chapter is a question you should not take lightly. Whether to file for bankruptcy is something that needs to be thought out, discussed, and not decided overnight. If you are not serious about bankruptcy, you should not file at this time. If you file and then voluntarily dismiss your case, or if the trustee or court dismisses your case for failing to do something required of you, then it greatly diminishes your chances at a successful bankruptcy at a later time.

Let us discuss the pros and cons of declaring bankruptcy.

The Pros

Protection from Creditors

First and foremost, filing for bankruptcy gives you protection from your creditors. This would eliminate those pesky calls at home and the embarrassing calls at work. On the other hand, most people do not know that you do not need to file bankruptcy to get your creditors off your back. You simply need to send them a letter telling them to leave you alone. By federal law, they have to stop harassing you, but that does not mean they will stop attempting to collect the debt. When the phone calls end, more often than not, the lawsuits begin. The creditors will sue you and attempt to garnish your wages. By filing bankruptcy, this will stop the creditors' garnishments.

The Automatic Stay

After filing your case, an "automatic stay" will be implemented. This prohibits your creditors from contacting you via phone or in writing, and also stops and prevents all wage garnishments. The automatic stay will also stop a public sale of your home, if your mortgage company is seeking foreclosure, and will prevent your vehicle from being repossessed. In some cases, if your car was just recently repossessed, it will be returned, although you will be held responsible for all the costs involved in storing and ultimately returning the vehicle to your possession.

Please note, automatic stays are not bulletproof. If you have filed a prior bankruptcy case in the 12-month period prior to the date of filing of the current case, the automatic stay will be in effect for only 30 days. In order for your creditors to not harass you and seek payment of their debts once again, you or your attorney must file a motion to extend the stay past the 30 days. The motion must provide reasons for the prior dismissal and list the changes in circumstances from your prior case for the judge to consider the motion. If it is granted, then the automatic stay is implemented for the life of the case, unless otherwise ordered.

If it is denied, you still may proceed with your bankruptcy case, but you will not be afforded the protection of the automatic stay. This means that you can continue in a Chapter 13 and attempt to repay your debts, but there is nothing to stop a creditor from seeking to foreclose on your home or repossess a vehicle. Most debtors voluntarily dismiss their cases at this point.

For an individual who has filed three or more cases in the prior 12-month period, the automatic stay is not implemented. Therefore, even though you have filed for bankruptcy, you do not have any real protection from your creditors. Again, you or your attorney must file a motion with the same type of provisions listed in a motion to extend the stay on a second case. This time, the motion would be to impose the automatic stay, and it is frequently filed as an emergency petition, so a hearing date is immediately granted. Many judges loathe granting an automatic stay in a third, fourth, or fifth case. These types of debtors are known as "serial filers," and it takes evidence to convince a judge that a debtor is serious about the process when he or she has two or more dismissed bankruptcy cases in the last year.

Even if you have filed a previous case more than one year ago, but less than two years prior, if in that prior case the automatic stay was denied or lifted, no stay will apply in the current case.

There is one more note on the automatic stay. A creditor can petition the judge for relief from the automatic stay at any point in the bankruptcy. Though, they have to provide a valid reason, for example: the debtor is not current (100 percent paid) on the trustee's records. You can contest this motion and the court will set a hearing date where you may state your case and the creditor will have to prosecute his motion. The judge will then render a ruling. If the ruling is in favor of you, then the automatic stay is still in effect. If the ruling is in favor of the creditor, then the automatic stay is no longer in effect as to that creditor, but the rest of your creditors are still held at bay with the automatic stay pertaining to them. But note that if the creditor that succeeded at lifting the automatic stay is your mortgage company or your car company, you risk losing your home to foreclosure and your vehicle to repossession, just like you did at the beginning of your bankruptcy.

You may wonder how the automatic stay can be a "pro" when there are so many of ways of it not being implemented or it being lifted. If you are committed to making your first bankruptcy work, make all your payments and comply with any orders of the court, you will succeed and your creditors will not have a valid reason to lift or attempt to deny you the automatic stay.

Discharge

Whether you file a Chapter 7 or Chapter 13, if you stay committed and complete your case, a "discharge," is issued. This means you have earned a clean slate.

All your credit card debts, hospitals bills, and any other unsecured debts are gone; you never have to worry about them again. Obviously, your mortgage and car payments will still need to be made, but any arrearages on those debts will have been paid in full in a Chapter 13. All back property taxes, water bills, and taxes older than three years will have been paid as well.

Some debts survive the discharge if they have not been paid in full during the Chapter 13 bankruptcy or wiped clean in a Chapter 7 bankruptcy. These debts are:

- Domestic support obligations: child support and/or alimony

- Student loans

- IRS debts less than three years old

- Criminal restitutions

- Debts incurred through fraud

The Cons

Sticking With It

If you chose to file or are ordered to convert to a Chapter 13, you are tied into a three- to five-year repayment plan. Sticking to a budget prior to filing was tough enough, but depending on your viewpoint, sticking to the same budget for three to five years will be even tougher with the oversight of the Bankruptcy Court on your finances.

You must petition the trustee and/or court for any purchase that exceeds $1,000. Therefore, if you have a two-year vehicle lease, you may need to ask permission two to three times for a new lease vehicle during the life of your plan. If you desire to take college courses that require obtaining a student loan, you must obtain approval for that as well. If you chose to refinance or sell your house while in bankruptcy, this too needs approval.

Also, if your bankruptcy case is dismissed and no discharge is granted, it may discourage you. Bankruptcy is not the only option to cure your credit ills, as we will discuss shortly, but it is commonly seen as the best, most viable option for giving people a fresh start. An unsuccessful case dumps people back into the same circumstances they faced before filing, and each successive case filed after the first is normally viewed with concern and pessimism on the part of the judge, trustees, and creditors.

Future Credit

When you file for bankruptcy, it will appear on your credit report for ten years. That is not to say you would not qualify for credit, it will just be more difficult. We will talk in Section III about how to deal with this, but you should know there are lasting effects, which could include higher interest rates. This is a "con," but a bankruptcy on your credit report is no more damaging than having several entries of unpaid debts that are in collections and have gone unpaid for years.

Public Record

Your bankruptcy is a matter of public record upon filing. In some areas, bankruptcies are listed in the newspapers, but these tend to be smaller papers, by and large focusing on the law. Even if it was in an upper echelon newspaper, when did you last look through the bankruptcy listings in your daily paper?

Honestly, this is not a big deal unless you are rich and famous. If you are an "average Joe" who has worked on the assembly line for 25 years, most likely, no one is going to search your name in the court records for a bankruptcy or scour the newspaper everyday waiting for the slight chance your name will appear. Even if they do, as we discussed in the introduction, bankruptcy is nothing to be ashamed of. Many people have filed, both famous and not-so-famous.

Other Options

Reading this book means you may have your heart set on filing bankruptcy, and that is your prerogative. Though, you should be fully aware that bankruptcy is not your only option. Before taking the leap into bankruptcy, it would be wise to explore all your options.

Attempt to Obtain Settlements

As a last ditch attempt to get payment before turning the debt over to a collections agency, many credit card companies will offer a settlement. After all the calls, letters, and threats, they feel they will almost certainly never get the full amount from you, so they will attempt to receive at least some of the debt. They will reduce your debt, sometimes by a great amount, if you pay the new figure in full immediately.

This may seem like a good idea, but the fact that you are considering bankruptcy undoubtedly means you do not have any excess income. To come up with, say, $5,000 to settle a $10,000 or more debt is, most likely, out of the question. Trying to get a personal loan or an additional credit card to pay this off is not a wise move. As we discussed in Chapter 1, obtaining additional credit to pay off an old bill is not a viable option.

You may approach your creditors asking them for a settlement, but this will yield the same results; payoff figures still be too steep to afford.

Ignore Your Debts

This is perhaps not the most ideal of circumstances, because you never know when a creditor will attempt to collect their debt again. As we discussed earlier, you do not need to file bankruptcy to stop your creditors from bothering you. You simply need to send them a letter asking them to cease all phone calls and letters, but chances are high you will be sued by the creditor. If you still do nothing, a court could issue a judgment requiring payment of the debt. This means garnishments on your wages and other types of income or assets. But there is only so much that creditors can take out of your paycheck to leave you a livable wage.

If all your assets are exempt, the creditors have nothing they can go after and cannot pursue repayment at this time. In Section II, we will discuss the exemptions in detail. These play a crucial role in bankruptcy cases.

If your assets are exempt and you ignore the situation, nothing will happen. The creditors will be frustrated, but they will wave the white flag – for now. You will be able to ease back into the everyday life you enjoyed before the calls began.

Nevertheless, eventually life will proceed as usual. A car will get old requiring many repairs or a new model, appliances will break, children will grow up, needing more expensive things like a car and college, and you will have no credit to help you finance these items.

People tend to change careers these days more than ever, so chances are, you will change jobs numerous times during your life. If you are fortunate enough to find a better paying job, those pesky creditors who you have not heard from in some time are watching and waiting. Making more money may move some of your property from the "exempt" category to "nonexempt," making that judgment you ignored years ago suddenly enforceable. Although they have appeared to go away, your creditors always watch your financial situation and will return to hounding you in a heartbeat.

Even if you decide to ignore all your debts, you should not ignore the IRS. If you owe the IRS back taxes, they will not sit idly by. They will use all recourses of the federal government to either charge you with a crime or, more likely, fine you. You do not need any more debts, especially to the IRS. The IRS is surprisingly willing to set up a payment plan with people who owe back taxes. This would also apply to state taxes.

Credit Counseling

With the exception of bankruptcy, this is almost certainly the most common solution for people with financial difficulties.

In this process, you will pay a monthly fee to meet with a credit counselor or a number of staff members of a credit counseling service, such as GreenPath. During the counseling session or series of sessions, you will be taught the fundamentals of having good credit: developing and sticking to a budget, managing your money better, and how to use credit for only the direst situations.

The credit counselor will also go over your current finances and contact your creditors on your behalf. The counselor will attempt to attain lower payment figures and come up with a working payment plan that you will be able to afford.

If each party is agreeable to the payment plan, you would pay the credit counselor, who in turn, disperses the funds to each creditor. When credit counseling programs work, you could possibly see progress on your credit report within a few months. Since you would have been making steady payments, the creditor would consider you current.

Conversely, credit counseling has distinct flaws. There is no obligation for creditors to participate and negotiate with credit counselors. So while some of your debts may be being paid through the credit counselor, others will still be left unpaid. If you are behind on a mortgage or a vehicle, the credit counselor will not deal with these types of debts. Even if the payment plan completes as it was agreed to, the creditor may still not be kind to your credit report. They may indicate the account was paid by a credit counseling firm, and this will appear on your credit report for over seven years.

Fees for credit counseling greatly range in price. Some charge a large deposit up front and then will lend you the money to pay their own fee. Not a smart move, as we have previously discussed.

One other thing to take note of with credit counseling: if your counselor is successful at reducing any one debt by over $600, the IRS takes notice. On the following year's tax return, you will owe taxes because the IRS now considers this income. This policy does not apply to bankruptcy, though.

If you choose this route, the key is to find the right credit counselor. Many counselors strive to help their clients. But like in any profession, there are counselors who see you only as another work task and do not go out of their way to rectify your situation. Worse yet, some counselors may have the creditors' interests in mind and steer you away from bankruptcy at all costs.

To find the right one, ask many informed questions before one cent leaves your wallet or purse.

Home Equity Loans

This is another popular, but flawed, way of attempting a debt recovery. What this essentially accomplishes is to take all your unpaid debts, such as credit cards and personal loans, and roll them into your mortgage payments.

This may seem like a good idea because all your creditors will be paid and will go away. Yet, now you have to pay more – albeit to only one source. This really does not reduce your debt, but just shovels it into everything else. If you were unable to pay all your debts before, you will not be able to now either. With the interest rate, you may end up paying even more in the long run, and your debt will hang with you for upwards of ten to fifteen years, depending on the terms of the loan.

It is possible that being in debt for so long and suddenly having credit again may send you into a shopping frenzy. It is only natural when sacrificing for so long to reward yourself when possible. But then one reward becomes two, and the rewards cost more and more; you may have been down this road before.

Before you know it, you are back to where you were before the home equity loan, but you are in worse shape because you now have to make that home equity loan payment too.

In some areas of the country these days, the housing market is in such bad shape that home equity loans are not even an option because the process involves taking the equity out of your home. Some people have seen the value of their houses decrease since they began owning the property. This would yield negative equity and would preclude those individuals from this option.

Mortgage Workout

Some banks or mortgage companies would be agreeable to taking the past due amount and putting it to the end of the mortgage. Some companies would jump at this chance, because it means extending the terms on the mortgage and increasing the amount it receives through the amount of interest gained.

This is only a viable option when this is the only debt in which you are behind, which is highly unlikely, because the mortgage is regularly the last thing people stop paying.

Making Your Decision

Now that you know what all your options are, it is time to decide whether bankruptcy is right for you. If you decide bankruptcy is not for you at this time, close this book and read no more. Come back to it if you change your mind or decide at a later date that it is time to file.

For those of you who have decided that bankruptcy is the path you would like to take, let us dive deeper into the world of bankruptcy by discussing your next steps before filing.

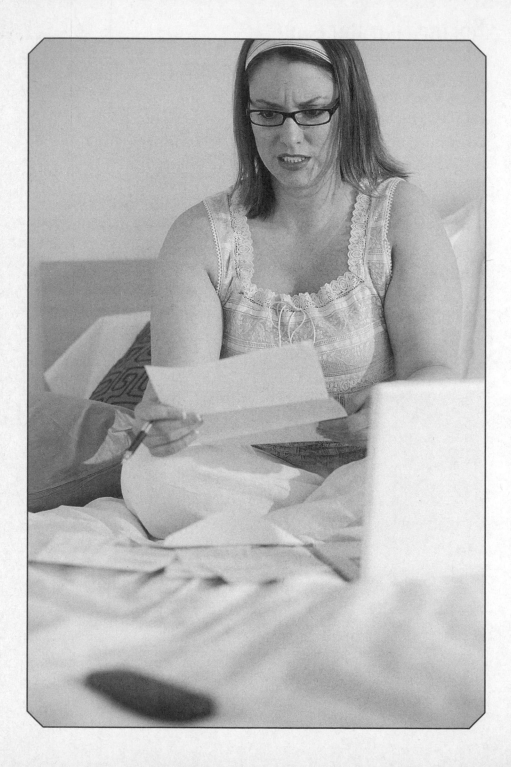

CHAPTER 3

Things To Do and Know Before Filing

"If the laws could speak for themselves, they would complain of the lawyers."
– Edward F. Halifax, British Politician

In most cases, if you have had a run-in with an attorney, it was a bad thing. Yet, in bankruptcy, many attorneys are out there to help you.

We will discuss our lawyer friends in this section, but first, you need to make sure your credit report is accurate.

You are most likely well-aware of who your creditors are, and roughly how much you owe to each, but chances are, you have never seen your own credit report. Before deciding on which type of bankruptcy is right for your situation and seeking the advice of a bankruptcy attorney, you should become extremely familiar with your credit report.

Pulling Your Credit Report

If you have never pulled your credit report, then you are able to get a copy for free. Actually, you are entitled to a free copy every year. If you have gotten your free copy for the year, the fee is nominal, on average around $10.

There are three ways of obtaining your free copy:

- Telephone: 877-322-8228

- Internet: **www.annualcreditreport.com**

- Mail: Annual Credit Report Service

   P.O. Box 105281

   Atlanta, GA 30348

Be sure to include your name, address, social security number, and date of birth with your request. The best way to receive a rapid response is by requesting a copy online. In most cases, you will receive your credit report in less than one day.

Your report will show all your credit, creditors, and who has asked for your credit report in the last two years. Take a hard look at your report, as many contain errors. Actually, a recent investigation by the United States Public Interest Research Group found that an incredible 70 percent of the credit reports they reviewed had at least one error contained in them.

Since they hound you incessantly and make you feel like less of a person, creditors may seem superhuman. But rest assured, they make mistakes, just like everyone else. This could be a data error when entering an account number or social security number. It could be that you have a common name, such as John Smith, and it got confused with the thousands of other "John Smiths," "Jon Smiths," and "Jon Smyths," among others.

Most people do not obtain their free credit report each year. Many people are denied credit for something appearing on their report that is false. Only when investigating their report after being denied for a purchase do these people discover these mistakes. This is a lesson you should carry with you after your bankruptcy has discharged. Check your report once a year, and if you can spare the extra money, do it twice per year.

When reviewing your report, make a separate list or highlight the portions on the report you feel are incorrect or inaccurate. If you have copies of your credit card statements, have those nearby so you can compare account numbers.

The following are some items that could appear on your report incorrectly:

- Your name, address, social security number, marital status, or birth date

- Incorrect or old employment information

- Bankruptcies older than ten years old

- Any credit checks older than two years and any credit checks from an automobile dealer for test driving a car (they can only run your credit if you initiate a purchase or a lease)

- Credits and lawsuits that do not belong to you

- Inaccurate payment status (meaning it indicates you paid late, when you paid on time)

- Missing notations of past written disputes of charges with creditors

- Collection agency listed separately from the creditor it purchased the debt from

- Accounts you closed appearing on your report as open

- Any account that is closed but does not state, "Closed by consumer." If this is not listed, it appears as if the creditor shut the account down

- Someone else's credit history with a similar name as yours

- Pre-marital debt of your spouse

- Voluntary surrender of a vehicle listed as a repossession

- Paid credit accounts, taxes, judgments, and other liens listed as unpaid

- Loans that inaccurately list you as a co-signer

Check and double check these, and notate anything you believe is wrong or inaccurate.

If you find inaccuracies or false information, you can send in the form provided with your credit report. You may submit the form via the Internet, but many inaccuracy claims require documentation to be submitted, and it may be easier to send it through the mail. You must provide enough documentation and clearly state your reasons for believing the falsehood for the bureau to investigate. If they deem the claim "frivolous," or do not have enough documentation to proceed with an investigation, they will drop the matter. Either way, you should receive a response within 30 to 45 days.

Now this will not help you when filing for bankruptcy in the near future, but at least you can take the copy of your credit report to your attorney and you can show him what you think your report should actually show. At this time, the attorney will most likely proceed with filing your plans and schedules to include some or all of the disputed information. If the investigation goes your way, the plans and schedules can be amended to remove these creditors.

Do I Need to Hire an Attorney?

At last we can get into the "meat and potatoes" of filing for bankruptcy. Everything that has preceded this has prepared you to file for bankruptcy, but now, we will get more into the specifics of the things you need to know and do before filing.

In Chapter 2, we told you had a big decision to make. If you are reading this, then you have decided to file for bankruptcy. Now you have a few other decisions to make before you file. The next decision is whether to seek the services of an attorney.

Anyone who has seen one of the numerous Law & Order marathons on television knows the age-old saying, "He who represents himself has a fool for a client." You are not a fool if you go it alone, but it is not a wise move.

Everyone has their opinion on attorneys, and even in bankruptcy, attorneys cost money. You can proceed with your case on your own by using this book and others to help you along. You can also pay some companies to prepare your petition and other documents needed to file. Nonetheless, once your case is filed, you are on your own to try to get it through the system.

Bankruptcy is a living, breathing entity. Judges are constantly rendering decisions that could affect your case, directly or indirectly, and the only way to have knowledge of these decisions is through an attorney. Not to mention, the pro-creditor bankruptcy reform laws passed by Congress and signed by the President in 2005 are still being interpreted by the bankruptcy community.

The number of "Pro Se" cases that are successfully confirmed or discharged is minuscule; there is just too much to know. You could file all your paperwork and think you have everything completed, but the court may dismiss your case because of a document you overlooked. If you are lucky or get the benefit of the doubt, and the missing document or documents go unnoticed by the court, the trustee, in most cases, will not hold your first hearing (the 341 Meeting) until these documents are filed, which could result in many days off of work for subsequent hearings and possible dismissal on a trustee motion if these documents are not filed. The trustee legally cannot advise you of which documents need to be filed because that would be seen as acting in favor of you, when they are supposed to be an independent agent between you and your creditors.

Also, know that if you do not employ an attorney, your creditors can still call you regarding your debts. As we discussed with the automatic stay, they are not allowed to contact you regarding your debts, but they can call your attorney, and they often do, regarding their treatment in the plan. The fact that you are representing yourself means the creditors can still call you.

The advantage of hiring an attorney in bankruptcy is the fact there are many bankruptcy attorneys to choose from. Most attorneys who advertise themselves as bankruptcy attorneys only do bankruptcy, or they are the lawyers who specialize in bankruptcies at their firms; these are the best attorneys to hire. If you have an attorney from a previous matter and want to use him, it is most likely a mistake. Many non-bankruptcy attorneys will not even attempt to file a bankruptcy for you. Instead, they will refer you to a lawyer specializing in bankruptcy. Bankruptcy takes a special breed of attorney who knows the bankruptcy code inside and out.

Attorney Fees

Unfortunately, it is hard to gauge what bankruptcy attorneys charge. Every district across the country allows a maximum amount of flat fees an attorney can charge for a Chapter 13. For example, in the Southeastern District of Michigan, which includes the Detroit Metropolitan area, the attorneys who file Chapter 13 cases can charge a maximum of $3,000.

But some attorneys seek what is called a fee application, which allows them to charge more than $3,000. However, this fee application must be approved by the trustee. If you have issues with the fee application, you may file objections and be heard before the judge. This, as you can imagine, just about kills the attorney-client relationship, and you may need to seek another attorney for any issues that arise in the future, such as your discharge.

These initial attorney fees commonly only cover from filing of the case through confirmation. If matters arise later, such as a motion to incur debt over $1,000 to lease a vehicle, or a creditor attempts to attain a motion to lift, additional charges will be sought. For these charges, an attorney must file a fee application to be reviewed by the trustee, and as before, if you have objections, you can be heard.

The good thing about the fees in a Chapter 13 case is that they are paid through the plan, meaning you will never have to directly pay for them. We will discuss Chapter 13 in depth soon, but the process is much like the credit counseling route we discussed in Chapter 2. You make a payment to the trustee, who in turn, disperses to all your creditors. The trustee takes a percentage for its servicing fee first to pay for its staff and necessary operating costs, then the attorney fees are taken out, followed by the debtor's creditors.

Chapter 7 cases range in price as well, often depending on how complicated your case is. In both Chapters, the attorney may want a deposit or a retainer before filing, and again, these tend to range in prices, but should rarely exceed $500. If this is your first bankruptcy case and an attorney wants more than $500 up front, you may want to look elsewhere. Yet, it is customary for some attorneys to charge more up front for debtors who have filed multiple cases because their odds of having a successful case decrease.

The key is to do your research. With any purchase, you want to be a smart consumer; hiring a bankruptcy attorney is no different. If you know someone who has filed bankruptcy before, ask them who they used and whether they would recommend that lawyer. Look in the phone book or on the Internet for attorneys. Call around to many different firms and ask a couple of questions before setting up an appointment. Do not just settle on one attorney immediately, unless someone gives you a glowing endorsement. Here are some good questions you may ask to find the best attorney:

- How much do you charge up front?

- If you intend to file a Chapter 7, ask: What will be my total cost?

- If you intend to file a Chapter 13, ask:

- Do you take a flat fee or intend to file a fee application?

- How much is your hourly rate if you charge me for post-confirmation work?

- What is your rate of confirmed cases in the past 12 months?

- What is your rate of discharged cases in the past three years?

These last two questions will catch many attorneys off guard. They will know you are extremely intelligent and are knowledgeable about the bankruptcy process.

"Confirmation" means that the court has deemed your Chapter 13 reorganization plan (or repayment plan) acceptable; you then begin paying back your creditors. If an attorney has a low confirmation rate, it could mean they are taking infeasible cases and are getting dismissed for this reason. It could also mean that the attorney is doing a poor job and not getting documents filed timely. Discharged cases, as we have previously discussed, refers to the amount of cases that have had all their debts repaid successfully, as proposed by their plan. This is another good barometer of this attorney's skills.

Non-Attorney Options

Non-Attorney Petition Preparers

One of the trickiest parts of declaring bankruptcy is the involved in filing. You may employ someone who will prepare your plans, schedules, and other necessary paperwork for a fraction of the cost of an attorney. Nevertheless, these are the only services these people can provide. The key word is "non-attorney," which means it is illegal for them to give legal advice. Once the paperwork is done, everything else is up to you. You must file these documents, represent yourself at all hearings, and answer all the trustee and creditor questions on your own.

Going Pro Se

This is simply doing everything on your own, including obtaining the proper forms, filling them out on your own, and filing them properly. Going it alone in a Chapter 7 may be possible, but you have got to know your stuff. Chapter 13 is a different matter, requiring three to five years of constant attention to the case and the need for an incredible knowledge of the bankruptcy code.

Types of Debts

Now let us discuss the differences in creditors during bankruptcy. We have referred to "secured" and "unsecured" debts previously and will refer to them again extensively in this book. Let us take a moment to describe the meaning of these classifications.

Secured Debts

Simply put, a secured debt is a something you will lose if you stop making payments. These debts are frequently backed by some sort of contract that you signed. When you were purchasing your house, you signed a contract. The fact that you are not paying means the creditor can reclaim the property. Since you are in bankruptcy, this action is prevented for the moment.

Here is a list of secured debts:

- Mortgages

- Home equity loans or second mortgages

- Loans for automobiles (including RVs, motorcycles, boats, ATVs, snowmobiles, and tractors)

- Stores claiming a secured interest on property, such as riding lawn mowers and large appliances. These are agreements made at the time of purchase between the department store and the purchaser that these purchases are secured property.

- Personal loans from a financial institution

- Judicial, statutory, or tax liens

Unsecured Debts

Most debts tend to be unsecured. This means there is no lien against property, you have not signed a security agreement, and the creditor has no real property to repossess.

Here are examples of the most common unsecured debts:

- Credit card purchases

- Store purchases without a security agreement

- Unpaid rent

- Loans from individuals, such as friends or relatives (unless a promissory note was signed offering a piece of collateral in exchange for non-payment)

- Health club / gym dues

- Accountant and attorney fees (not including your

current attorney's fees, although this would include fees owed to an attorney on a prior bankruptcy)

- Religious fees

- Union dues

- Utility bills (not including water, which is a secured lien on your home)

Student loans are also technically considered unsecured, but they survive discharge. As we discussed above, this means despite all your other debts being wiped out at discharge, this one will remain, unless you provide good cause for an exception. If you file a Chapter 13 and offer, say 50 percent to your unsecured creditors, that means that after discharge, you still have to pay off the rest of the student loan. Your bankruptcy will have paid off half of your student loan debt, and even though you owe nothing more on the rest of your unsecured debts after discharge, you still must pay the other half of your student loan debt.

Priority Debts

There is a third debt we have not talked about yet, and that is the priority debt. Technically referred to as "priority unsecured," these debts are considered unsecured but have "priority" over the rest of the unsecured creditors, and as such, get paid prior to the rest of those debts in a Chapter 13. No matter what percentage is offered to the unsecured creditors, these creditors receive everything they are owed. In a Chapter 7, these are frequently the first creditors to receive proceeds from the sale of non-exempt property.

These debts tend to be:

- All compensation owed to any employees if you are a business owner

- Debts not exceeding $10,800 ($5,400 to each) owed to farmers or fisherman

- Debts up to $2,425 in deposits provided for each case of services promised but not delivered to non-business entities, such as homeowners and other private individuals

- Income taxes less than three years old

As with unsecured debts, some priority debts survive discharge. These are child support, alimony, divorce agreements or judgments, and other domestic support obligations. Even though they are receiving 100 percent of what they are owed, some debts are too large to be paid through a Chapter 13 plan, and a balance will be left over after discharge.

Special Unsecured

There is a fourth kind of debt, but it is rare. Some debtors chose to protect someone who helped them out by being a co-signer on a debt. More often than not, this is to protect a parent who co-signed on a credit card for a child attending college for the first time. This will prevent the creditor from going after the co-signer for your debt because they cannot get it from you in bankruptcy. These creditors are paid 100 percent of what they are owed and, in most cases, will be paid off by the discharge.

Determining Your Income

It is important to sit down and determine your monthly income, especially if you are proceeding without an attorney. This has an immense effect on whether you will be able to file a Chapter 7, or, if you want or need to file for a Chapter 13, whether your case will last three or five years.

In the next few chapters, we will discuss where these numbers fit in, but for now, it is important for you to accurately figure out your monthly income for the past six months. We use six months because this is now the standard brought about by the recent bankruptcy changes. When the bankruptcy trustee inquires about your current monthly income, what they are asking for is your average monthly income for the prior six-month period.

Six-Month Look-Back Period

When determining this, it is important to know what exactly the "look-back period" is. The last day of the six-month look-back period is determined to be the final day of the month preceding your filing. Then you will look back at all your earned income for six months back to the first day of the month six months ago.

For example, if you file for bankruptcy on July 8, your look-back period would end on June 30 and date back to January 1. So, your look-back period would be from January 1 through June 30. If you filed for bankruptcy on March 29, your look-back period would be September 1 through February 28 (or 29, if it is a leap year).

Types of Income Determined in the Calculation

Nearly every monetary source you received in the last six months must be considered income and figured into your calculation.

These income sources are:

- Any gross revenue received from employment (including tips, bonuses, overtime, commissions, and profit sharing)

- Net income from operation of a business or self-employment (Please note, this figure is net, not gross. Where the above wages are listed as a gross figure, small businesses are given the benefit of subtracting reasonable expenses before reporting this income.)

- Interest, dividends (such as proceeds from a stock sale or retirement account cash-out), and royalties (lotto or gambling winnings and inheritances)

- Rent (again, a net figure)

- Pension, retirement, unemployment, disability, and worker's compensation

- Contributions from other people residing in household (such as children, significant other, or fiancé)

- Contributions from a person not residing in household for you or people in the household (such as child support and alimony)

There are two exceptions in which you do not have to count money received as income. They are:

- Social security (retirement or disability)

- Payments to victims of war crimes or terrorism (i.e., the widows and families of the victims of the September 11th terrorism attacks do not have to report this as income)

Calculate

To figure out this income, you should gather together all copies of your pay stubs, bank statements, pension income verification, and any other statement that shows your wages for the prior six months. It is crucial that you keep these documents in a folder or somewhere you can quickly find them. If you hire an attorney, they will need to review these documents, and they need to be submitted to the trustee as well.

Now add together all your pay stubs over the last six-month period, taking into account the proper look-back period (do not go back too far or include stubs of the current month). Next, add to this figure any income received from any other source, excluding only social security (and the rare exception for victims of terror and war crimes). Then, add these all together and divide by six, and you will have your current monthly income figure.

Example

To give you a better understanding of how to plug in these numbers, here is an entirely fictional example. As they say on television and the movies, "any similarities are strictly coincidental."

Let us get familiar with the Johnson family. We will use them as an example family often in the next few chapters to show you how they would file the very complicated paperwork if they, like you, were filing for bankruptcy.

Jim and Judy Johnson are about to file bankruptcy and want to figure out what their currently monthly income figure is so they can match it to the state median income figure (we will discuss this in the next chapter). The couple sits down on April 19 and figures out all their income for the past six months by using the list we laid out above:

Jim and Judy Johnson's Income (October 1 through March 31)

1. Any gross revenue received from employment (including tips, bonuses, overtime, commissions, and profit sharing)

Jim is a salaried employee, so his monthly income is the same every month. Judy is in retail, is paid hourly, and does not have set hours, so her income varies from month to month, but picks up around the holidays. Wages are listed as gross.

	Jim	Judy
October	$ 4,500	$ 1,892
November	$ 4,500	$ 2,016
December	$ 4,500	$ 2,589
January	$ 4,500	$ 1,990
February	$ 4,500	$ 1,746

	Jim	Judy
March	$ 4,500	$ 1,809
Total	$ 27,000	$ 12,042
Total for both	$39,042	

2. Net income from operation of a business or self-employment

Judy makes arts and crafts in her spare time and sells them at local craft shows. She has to pay for a table at most of the shows and for the material. Some months are better than others, and she makes a profit or breaks even, others, she pays more for the materials and tables than she brings in.

Month	Profit
October	$ -495
November	$ 275
December	$ - 32
January	$ 475
February	$ 0
March	$ 28
Total	$ 251

3. Interest, dividends, and royalties

Jim sold some stocks last July, but since it is not in the look-back period, he does not count it. The couple had no other income in this category.

Total $0

4. Rent

Jim's mother resides in the household and pays $500 each month for rent, except for December. As part of her Christmas present, Jim & Judy told her not to pay rent for the month of December.

Month	Rent
October	$ 500
November	$ 500
December	$ 0
January	$ 500
February	$ 500
March	$ 500
Total	$ 2,500

5. Pension, retirement, unemployment, disability, and worker's compensation

The couple did not have any income in this category.

Total $ 0

6. Contributions from other people residing in household

The Johnsons have two children, Jack and Jill, who are ten and three years old respectively. Obviously, neither provide support. Jim's mother receives social security from which she pays her rent, but she does not contribute anything else to the household.

Total $ 0

7. Contributions from a person not residing in household for you or people in the household

Judy was married before and Jack is her child from that marriage. Judy is entitled to receive child support for Jack. She used to be entitled to alimony as well, but upon marrying Jim, she was no longer entitled to this income. She is now only entitled to child support but receives it only sporadically and not always for the full amount of $650.

Month	Income
October	$ 180
November	$ 0
December	$ 650
January	$ 650
February	$ 0
March	$ 275
Total	$ 1,755

8. Total of Items 1-7

Number of Items	Income
1.	$ 39,042
2.	$ 251
3.	$ 0
4.	$ 2,500
5.	$ 0
6.	$ 0
7.	$ 1,755
Total	$ 43,548

$43,548 represents what the Johnsons' combined income was for the last six months. The one step left and that is to divide this number by six, the number of months for this income.

9. Total of Items 1-7 divided by six months

$43,548/6=$7,258

$7,258 is Jim & Judy Johnson's current monthly income. They can now match that to the state median income level and decide what their options are at that point.

We have now discussed some important, necessary components of the bankruptcy process and calculated your income. It is now time to differentiate between the most common types of consumer bankruptcies, Chapters 7 and 13.

CHAPTER 4

Types of Bankruptcy

"Capitalism without bankruptcy is like Christianity without Hell."
– Frank Borman, American Astronaut and business executive

Despite what Mr. Borman thinks, you are not a bad person for filing bankruptcy. You are being proactive with your situation, and that is laudable. You have chosen this avenue, and now it is time to explore bankruptcy by looking at which bankruptcy you can file. If you hire an attorney, you may want him or her to determine which type of bankruptcy is right for you. Though, you may already have a preference.

Here is an overview of the types of bankruptcy you can file.

Chapter 7

The most common bankruptcy is described in Chapter 7 of Title 11 in the United States Code, hence the term "Chapter 7." This is sometimes called the "liquidation" bankruptcy, meaning the Chapter 7 bankruptcy trustee is responsible for selling (or liquidating) your non-exempt assets. We will discuss what you can exempt later.

People who have much secured debt or are not current on their homes and vehicles should not file for Chapter 7. In a Chapter 13, people are allowed to keep these types of properties, as long as they become current and cure the arrearages during the life of the plan. In a Chapter 7 case, if these properties are not current, they will be sold by the trustee.

Eligibility

Pretty much anyone can file for a Chapter 7. There is no debt limit and you need not be employed to file for this type of bankruptcy. Due to the lack of a debt ceiling, some corporations file for a Chapter 7 over a Chapter 11. The reason for corporations choosing a Chapter 7 is much the same as a consumer deciding between Chapter 7 and 13. A Chapter 7 is a quick process compared to a Chapter 11 or 13, albeit a much longer process for a business than an individual. A Chapter 7 liquidates the corporation's and the individual's debts, whereas a Chapter 11 or 13 will restructure debts and come up with a repayment plan.

Chances are good that you are not a CEO of a company reading this book to decide which bankruptcy to file. After all, they have high-priced attorneys and advisors to make those decisions for them, so we will stick to discussing you, the individual.

Fees

In addition to any attorney fees, there are a couple of other fees involved in the bankruptcy process. In Chapter 7, you will pay a $299 filing fee to the court. In certain cases, a waiver for the fees may be obtained, but this is exceedingly rare. The more common way to soften the blow of this fee is to pay this debt in installments. An application may be obtained from your area bankruptcy court's Web site, and these applications are rarely turned down.

The Role of the Chapter 7 Trustee

One downside to filing for Chapter 7 protection when you have assets that need liquidating is that you obtain another creditor. The trustee's role in a Chapter 7 is to explore your finances and sell any property. This is because the trustee receives a commission on the selling price of each item. Obviously, this may not matter if you have come to terms with your property being sold.

Conversely, if all your assets are exempt, the trustee will not take much issue in your case, and you will only encounter him at your hearing, described below.

Credit Counseling

One of the reforms of the 2005 Bankruptcy Reform Act was to require every debtor who files for bankruptcy, regardless of which Chapter they are filing under, to seek credit counseling. Each state has a list of approved credit counselors. Since every state has a different list, it would be best to ask your attorney. Many times, the attorney works with a particular credit counselor for all his cases, so you will not have to choose. If you are proceeding without counsel, you can determine which credit counselors are approved in your state by logging on to **http://www.usdoj.**

gov/ust and clicking on "Credit Counseling and Debtor Education."

This particular credit counseling is a little different than the credit counseling program we discussed in Chapter 2. It is simply two sessions, one before filing and one while your case is pending.

The first session must take place no more than 180 days prior to the filing of the bankruptcy case, although some courts look for these sessions to have taken place on the same day in which your bankruptcy case was filed, or the day before. To be on the safe side, you may want to consider waiting until the day of or the day before filing to take part in the session. This session is a simple consultation in which the counselor will determine whether there is a feasible way to restructure or minimize your debt before proceeding to a bankruptcy. The fact that you are on the eve of filing bankruptcy means that a non-bankruptcy restructuring plan is most likely not a viable option. Even if the counselor suggests there is another way to handle your debt, you are not bound by the decision. The credit counseling agency will issue you a certificate, and you must include this certificate with the rest of your bankruptcy documents when filing with the court. Failure to take part in this credit counseling, or to file the certificate, may result in the dismissal of your case before your first hearing.

The second session will take place while your case is pending, likely after your court hearing. The purpose of this session is to provide a personal financial management tutorial before you are released from the protection bankruptcy offers. To get a discharge, you must provide proof that you completed this portion. Failure to obtain this proof may result in dismissal of your case.

Being exempt from pre-bankruptcy credit counseling is extremely rare. You must petition the court for excusal for "exigent circumstances." Residents in the New Orleans area had been exempt because of Hurricane Katrina until March 2008 when this exception was terminated.

Fees are normally $50 per session for a total of $100 per case. Some credit counselor agencies will ask that both sessions be paid up front during the first session. Others will allow you to pay for the second session at the time you participate in it. If your situation is dire enough, you may be able to get the credit counselor to waive your fee, but again, this is rare.

Means Test

The catch to filing a Chapter 7 case is that you must pass the Means Test to qualify. The Means Test is simply a form into which you plug some numbers to determine whether you have enough disposable income after deducting a certain number of allowances to allow repayment to your creditors. Your current monthly income must be less than your state's median income for you to be able to file for a Chapter 7 without having to complete the Means Test. If your disposable income shows an ability to pay some money back to your creditors, you will be forced to file a Chapter 13. Refer back to Chapter 3 to determine your current monthly income to compare it with your state's median income.

To determine your state's median income level, go to: **http://www.usdoj.gov/ust/eo/bapcpa/meanstesting. htm.**

Please be aware that these numbers change about twice per year. To get the most accurate numbers, you will have to toggle a drop down menu and click on the timeline that reflects your filing date. The number varies by the number of people in your household.

We will go into a more detailed discussion of how to fill out the Means Test in Section II.

Court Hearings

For most Chapter 7 cases, only one court hearing is held. This hearing is most commonly referred to as the "341 Meeting," or "341 Hearing," but could also be called the "341 First Meeting of Creditors," or simply, "The First Meeting of Creditors." This hearing is held by the trustee who is assigned to your case. The hearing is normally not held in a court room, but in a smaller conference or meeting room, and no judge is present. The trustee will ask you a series of questions on the pleadings contained in your documents. Your creditors receive a notice for this hearing and have a right to appear and ask you questions, but in most cases, they do not appear, and the trustee will be the only party asking you questions. If you have filed all your documents truthfully and accurately, this will be a fairly painless process.

If all goes well, you will not have to appear in court again, but this is not guaranteed.

Here are some situations that will necessitate a hearing in front of a judge:

- Income on your documents shows you are ineligible for Chapter 7, in which case you (or your attorney) will have to argue for an exception to be made for your case

- The trustee or a creditor contends your income is too high to file Chapter 7

- Seeking a judge's approval to discharge a frequently non-dischargeable debt

- Removing a lien that will survive post-discharge

- You are seeking a "reaffirmation agreement for secured debts," which means you want to "reaffirm" the contract by continuing the proper payments

There are other issues that may have to be heard before a judge, but the above occurrences are the most common.

Dismissal

Do not get the terms "dismissal" and "discharge" confused. Sometimes, people think "case dismissed" is a good thing because when a criminal court case is dismissed, it means the defendant is free to go. "Dismissal" means your case has been deemed infeasible, or a number of other issues have occurred, such as failure to attend your 341 Meeting or other court hearings. The court will then dismiss, or terminate, the case. This will stop your bankruptcy case, the automatic stay will cease, and your creditors will be once again free to come after you for payment.

Many times, if a dismissal for ineligibility (not passing the Means Test) is being sought on a case, the trustee will ask for dismissal or conversion to Chapter 13. If, at the hearing, you do not successfully argue for an exception for your case, it will be up to the judge whether to dismiss or convert your case. Most of the time, judges will allow you to convert your case and attempt a repayment plan in a Chapter 13, as opposed to totally dismissing your case.

You may wish to dismiss your case on your own at any time. Though, in a Chapter 7 case, they do not have to honor this request. If you have an asset or assets that can be liquidated, the Chapter 7 will be in the best interests of your creditors, and you will not be allowed to dismiss the case.

If you do successfully dismiss your case, or your case is dismissed, you are able to file again. Yet, in some cases, you have to wait 180 days (6 months) to re-file. In any re-filed case, you will have to pay another court fee, and in many cases, obtain and pay for new credit counseling. You also have the right to request your case be converted to a Chapter 13.

Discharge

This is what you are striving for: a discharge. When you receive a discharge, this means your Chapter 7 case has been successfully closed, the debts you owed have been wiped clean, and the creditor can never again attempt to collect this debt or report it as unpaid on your credit report.

Some debts, on the other hand, can never be wiped away in a Chapter 7. They are:

- Domestic support obligations (child support, alimony, or divorce agreements and/or judgments)

- Fines and surcharges relating to felonies, misdemeanors, infractions, contempt of court charges, or restitution

- Income taxes less than three years old or any taxes that were deemed as a deliberate attempt to avoid payment

- Property, payroll, and other taxes

- Association fees

- Retirement plan loans (such as 401k loans)

- Debts where discharge in a prior case was attempted and dismissed for fraud, abuse, or bad acts

- Any debt a creditor successfully argues not be discharged

In rare cases, student loans can be discharged if you can prove an exception applies. This would be based on three factors: poverty, hardship, and good faith (meaning you attempted to pay these debts).

Chapter 13

There are more difference than similarities between a

Chapter 13 and a Chapter 7. The big advantage Chapter 13 has over Chapter 7 is that your non-exempt assets will not be sold. The reason for this is that you are proposing a prepayment plan for your creditors. The secured creditors will receive everything they are owed while the unsecured debts may be paid everything, nothing, or some of what was owed, depending on your income. Most cases last at least three years while others continue for five.

Similarities

We described the Chapter 7 process above; here are the similarities when filing for a Chapter 13.

Credit Counseling

Since the 2005 Bankruptcy Reform Laws, everyone seeking the protection of bankruptcy must seek out credit counseling no more than 180 days prior to filing, but preferably, one day before filing or the actual day of filing. Refer to the above information to obtain the approved credit counseling agencies in your state.

Fees are the same: $50 per session, $100 for both sessions. The only real difference between the types of bankruptcies here is when the second session is taken. As we talked about before, barring any major issues, a Chapter 7 is a fairly straightforward, short process. The second session is frequently held within a month or two of the first because a Chapter 7 case, more often than not, runs its course in two to three months. Conversely, Chapter 13 is a long process that could stretch from three to five years. The second session is by and large taken just prior to discharge, so it theoretically could take place several years after the first session.

Means Test

You do not have to pass the Means Test to be eligible for a Chapter 13 case, but, as with a Chapter 7, you still must complete it.

As we stated above, the Means Test will be discussed in depth later on, as this chapter is just an overview of the types of bankruptcy. Unlike a Chapter 7, which determines your eligibility, a Chapter 13 Means Test determines the length of your plan.

If your current monthly income is less than your state's median income, you do not have to complete the Means Test, and you may propose a three-year repayment plan. If your current monthly income is more than your state's median income, you must complete the Means Test and, in most instances, your case must run five years. Refer to the link and instructions for finding the state median income in the Chapter 7 Means Test section.

Dismissal

As with a Chapter 7, a Chapter 13 bankruptcy case can be dismissed at any time for almost any reason. Because a Chapter 13 has a much longer process, the odds of your case being dismissed increase. Therefore, you must always be diligent and answer all letters, calls, and inquires from the Chapter 13 trustee and your attorney, as they may be contacting you to advise you of a potential situation that could result in a dismissal. By ignoring these correspondences, or not participating in any hearings, your case will most likely be dismissed.

In a Chapter 13, a case could be dismissed for a variety of reasons. Here are some of the most common:

- Failure to attend any hearing

- You have been terminated or quit your job without telling your attorney or the trustee, and you stop making payments

- Failure to comply with an order from the court

- Your case has been deemed infeasible by the judge

- Poor payment history or zero pay

- Documents missing or submitted incomplete when originally filing the case

As with a Chapter 7, in a Chapter 13, you may dismiss your case at any time, and in rare cases, if you meet the requirements, you can convert to a Chapter 7. Once your case is dismissed, you are free to re-file your case unless your creditors or the trustee has successfully argued before the judge that you be barred from filing another case for 180 days, or six months. In almost every first case, this does not happen. This measure is reserved for debtors who have filed multiple cases each time their home is about to be foreclosed upon. This gives the mortgage company a chance to reclaim their property.

If your prior case was within a one-year period, you or your attorney must file a motion to extend or impose the automatic stay. We discussed this procedure in detail in Chapter 1.

Discharge

After three to five years, if you have met the conditions of your plan, your case is discharged, and the debts you had are either paid in full or paid as much as was promised. The creditor can never again attempt to collect this debt or report it as unpaid on your credit report. All the debts listed as non-dischargeable in the Chapter 7 section are non-dischargeable in a Chapter 13, with one notable exception: nonsupport divorce debts. These do not include alimony and child support, which are always non-dischargeable.

Differences

Now let us focus on the differences between Chapter 7 and Chapter 13.

Eligibility

According to the United States Courts Web site (**http://www.uscourts.gov**), the eligibility for a Chapter 13 is as follows:

Any individual, even if self-employed or operating an unincorporated business, is eligible for Chapter 13 relief as long as the individual's unsecured debts are less than $336,900 and secured debts are less than $1,010,650. 11 U.S.C. § 109(e). These amounts are adjusted periodically to reflect changes in the consumer price index. A corporation or partnership may not be a Chapter 13 debtor.

You must also have filed all income tax returns required prior to filing your case. If and when it is discovered these are not filed, the trustee and/or court have the right to dismiss your case without a hearing.

Fees

Slightly less expensive than a Chapter 7, it costs $274 in court costs to file a Chapter 13. As in a Chapter 7, a debtor can seek to have his court fees paid in installments.

Chapter 13 Trustee

The Chapter 13 trustee is the kinder, gentler trustee. Unlike the Chapter 7 trustee, this trustee has no personal stake in your case. They do get paid, anywhere from 5 to 10 percent of your payments, but this is strictly for logistical reasons to cover operational costs. In other words, the Chapter 13 trustee is not going to make a profit on your case.

The Chapter 13 trustee has many duties that the Chapter 7 does not. They play a more active role in cases that the Chapter 7 trustee would be virtually nonexistent in.

Here are their basic duties:

- Review and verify many components of your proposed plan

- Disperse the payments you make to them to your creditors in the appropriate order

- Make sure you file all income tax returns at the beginning, end, and during the case

- Notify any child support recipients and agencies you may be obligated to that you have filed bankruptcy

The trustee will frequently leave you alone if you are making all your payments, filing your tax returns and submitting any refunds you agreed to and not changing jobs or having an increase in income. You may have to contact your trustee if you need to buy or lease a new car or obtain credit during the life of your plan.

If you get an incredible new job, a large raise, win the lotto, receive a monetary judgment from a lawsuit, or receive a substantial buyout of your employment, the trustee may seek to have your plan amended to provide for all your creditors to receive 100 percent of their debts.

Court Hearings

In an ideal Chapter 13 case, there should only be two court hearings in which you need to appear – the 341 Meeting or Hearing and the Confirmation Hearing.

We discussed the 341 Meeting in the Chapter 7 section. This is just about the same hearing for both forms of bankruptcy. It is commonly held about five to six weeks after you have filed your case. You must appear at this hearing, as the trustee will be asking you questions about the documents you filed with the court and any other questions they may have about your financial affairs. Again, your creditors are invited to attend but rarely do so. Even if they do appear, they must be cordial with you or face a rebuke by the trustee holding the hearing.

If you cannot attend this hearing because you cannot get out of work (or any other unavoidable emergency) on the scheduled date, you need to contact your attorney or the trustee as soon as possible. In most cases, if you let the parties know early that you cannot attend, they will give you another date. But if you just do not show up without telling anyone prior to the hearing, your case will most likely be dismissed. You should use this rule of thumb for any Chapter 13 hearing, including the Confirmation hearing.

The purpose of the 341 Meeting in a Chapter 13 is to allow the trustee and creditors to ask you any questions that have arisen from their review of your plan and other documents you filed with the court. After the hearing, the trustee will file objections they may have with your plan, and it is up to you and your attorney (or yourself, if you are a Pro Se debtor) to answer these objections. You will either amend them to comply with the trustee's wishes or argue against the trustee's objections at your next hearing – the Confirmation Hearing.

Typical trustee objections can be:

- Bad faith. This can stem from a variety of things, such as filing multiple cases, inaccuracy in filings and testimony, the inability to offer anything to unsecured creditors, or deliberately attempting to circumvent a judicial ruling.

- Plan is infeasible or the inability to make the required payments with the current budget.

- The best interest of the creditor is not met. This means your creditors are required to receive as much as they would have if you filed for a Chapter 7. Therefore, the proceeds from the liquidated non-exempt property must be roughly the same as or less than the amount that will be paid back in a Chapter 13.

- Discrimination between creditors. For example, to

make life at the Thanksgiving dinner table easier, you may want to pay back your uncle 100 percent of what he loaned you, but his debt is considered an unsecured debt. Thus, if you are offering 20 percent to all other unsecured debts, such as your Capital One card, you cannot pay back your uncle 100 percent.

- Not providing for adequate protection. Under the new code, secured creditors with collateral, such as automobiles, must be afforded equal monthly payments.

If your 341 Meeting is concluded, then you may proceed to the Confirmation Hearing, which is regularly scheduled five to six weeks later. Conversely, if your 341 case was held open for any reason, or adjourned and not officially concluded, your Confirmation Hearing cannot be held.

The Confirmation Hearing will be in a courtroom before a judge. At that time, the judge will decide whether your case is plausible or infeasible. The judge may accept your plan by confirming it, deny confirmation for the moment, tell you to amend your plan for various reasons, and adjourn your Confirmation Hearing to a later date, or the judge may reject your plan altogether because it is infeasible (meaning you do not have enough income to pay all your secured and priority debts in full). If the judge rejects your case, your case will be dismissed.

After the Confirmation Hearing (or last Confirmation Hearing, if it is adjourned one or more times), you may or may not have to appear in court again.

Here are some possible reasons you will end up in court again:

- To amend your plan if your income increases or decreases significantly after confirmation

- To respond to a motion by a creditor or the trustee to dismiss your case

- To respond to a motion by a creditor to lift the stay on a piece of property, such as your home or car

- As in a Chapter 7, if you seek approval to discharge a normally non-dischargeable debt

- If the trustee or creditor attempts to deny your discharge for some reason

Chapters 11 and 12

These are options for individuals, but characteristically, they are reserved for a select group of people.

Chapter 11 is frequently the protection businesses seek when reorganizing their debts. Normally, large corporations will seek Chapter 11 while small businesses will file for Chapter 7, or occasionally, Chapter 13. Individuals who are not eligible for Chapter 13 (exceeding $336,000 of unsecured and $1,010,650 of secured debts) occasionally seek the protection of a Chapter 11; though, the process is extremely cost inhibitive. The initial filing fee is over $800, and quarterly fees are required. Attorney fees are exorbitant in a Chapter 11, and most charge retainers, which approach $10,000.

A Chapter 12 case is the doppelganger of the Chapter 13 process. Though, to be eligible, the vast majority of your debts must come from the operation of a family farm. This book discusses only the Chapter 7 and 13 processes. If you are a farmer or a large corporation, you should seek the advice of an attorney or a different book.

We have now discussed the similarities, differences, and eligibility requirements of the two major types of bankruptcies, and now it is time to file.

In Section II, we will begin to discuss the nuts and bolts of bankruptcy in further detail, such as how to file your paperwork and what will be needed to have your case considered complete. We will go more in depth with many of the subjects discussed in this section, which was designed to give you a cursory knowledge of the bankruptcy process.

Now it is time to master your knowledge of the process.

PART II

YOUR BANKRUPTCY CASE

CHAPTER 5

Filing The Proper Paperwork

"We can lick gravity, but sometimes the paperwork is overwhelming."
– *Wernher Von Braun, German Rocket Pioneer*

No one likes paperwork. Sadly, in bankruptcy, there is no way around filling out a large amount of paperwork.

The following chapter will describe the various forms of paperwork needed and how to fill it out. If you are a Pro Se debtor, it is vital that you learn the proper way to complete and file these documents.

If you have employed an attorney, it is still crucial to know this information. Your lawyer will fill this information out for you, but you need to review and sign the documents before the attorney files them with the court. If the lawyer does not show you the documents and instead asks you to sign a blank sheet of paper or tells you not to worry about reviewing your documents, firmly ask to read them over anyway. **Do not sign anything you have not thoroughly read.** Remember, this is your case, not your attorney's. The attorney will not be the one losing his house if your case goes south because something was not filed correctly.

With that in mind, we will begin this chapter by discussing what you do on your first consultation with your attorney. If you are going it alone, skip this section and move on to the sections about filing the proper documents.

First Meeting with Your Attorney

This may be the first meeting you have at the law firm, or it could possibly be the second. In some cases, paralegals will meet with you for an initial consultation because the attorney may be in court on other matters. Do not feel you are getting the "brush off" if this is the case. This is standard operations for many firms who only have one bankruptcy attorney or an attorney who is in business by himself and not employed by a firm. The paralegal may give you a questionnaire and/or ask about your finances. They will also advise you of the documents you need to bring with you for your next visit.

If this is the route your bankruptcy attorney takes, you almost certainly do not need all your documents at this time, but do not make this assumption. When scheduling the first appointment, you should inquire about which documents are needed at this first meeting and whether you will be seeing a lawyer.

Some attorneys will want to get right down to business and ask you to bring all relevant documents to the first meeting. If this is the case, again, be sure to ask what documents your attorney needs.

Here are some of the most common things an attorney will need:

- Your credit report

- Copies of your four most recently filed tax returns (although two years is also acceptable)

- At least 60 days of pay stubs for you and for your spouse, regardless of whether they are filing with you

- Verification of income received through pension and social security

- If self-employed or running a business: business statements, bank statements, bills for expenses, and any other business-related documents

- Deeds to real estate owned or a rental agreement if renting

- Appraisal information on your home

- Titles and approximate values on any vehicles owned

- Paperwork on your debts, whether it be credit card statements, student loan agreements, or any unpaid government debt documents (such as unpaid tax letters)

- Information on child support, alimony, and divorce proceedings (bring a divorce judgment if you have one)

- Information regarding any lawsuits you have filed or

that have been filed against you and any garnishments being deducted from your paycheck

Some lawyers will want you to create a budget of your monthly expenses and bring that with you. Others will provide a form at the appointment and the two (or three) of you will go over it together. Also, be sure to advise attorneys if you have filed for bankruptcy in the past.

Tips for Dealing with Your Attorney

Be Open and Honest with Your Attorney

This is not the time to be evasive or embarrassed to tell your whole story. If you leave out any detail, even if you think it is a minor detail, it could be detrimental to your case. It also makes your lawyer look bad if the trustee, creditor, or judge discovers a missing detail later in the case. Even if you did not inform them of these issues, it may be seen as though your attorney is not doing his job. Lawyers do not like to look bad.

Do not be Intimidated: Ask Questions

Upon entering the office, you may notice that the lawyer may have numerous degree and awards on their walls. They could even have pictures of themselves with famous people, like the President of the United States. This can be extremely intimidating when you may already be a little upset with yourself that you have had to go down this road, combined with the fact that this person has so much education and success. You may feel that the attorney will look down his nose at you and your situation.

These sentiments are natural, but you need to sweep them out of your mind immediately. The attorney is not a better person than you because he, along with thousands of others, paid $3,000 to have dinner with the President and have his picture taken afterward. You can amuse yourself by thinking a few more dinners like that and your attorney will be filing for bankruptcy as well. The truth is, if it were not for you and people like you, the attorney would not have a job. He owes it to you to be cordial and understanding of your situation.

Do not allow yourself to be intimidated or too scared to ask any important questions you may have. As we said before, this is your bankruptcy, not your attorney's. Your attorney shuts his light off and goes home every night to his own problems. If your case gets dismissed for something you did not understand, and did not question, they may feel sympathy toward you, but ultimately, they have to go on with their other cases.

Even if you feel it may be a "dumb" question, or one your lawyer has heard thousands of times, ask it anyway. You are paying him to listen and answer your questions.

Remember You are Now Employing this Attorney

An attorney's job is to advise you of the correct way to go about your bankruptcy, but if at any time you feel he is not doing a good job, you can seek a new attorney. This is not always the most desired option because if the case is filed, and afterward, you decide you want a different attorney, you will owe fees to this attorney and the next one you hire. You need to use your best judgment in the initial consultation and gauge whether this is the correct attorney for you. If not, inform the attorney you have changed your mind and move on to the attorney that was second on your list. Most times, you will not owe anything for the initial consultation, and are free to change your mind.

If you were a boss, and you had an employee talking down to you and being rude, most likely, you would fire this employee. Remember, you are in the "boss" role in the attorney-client relationship. You do not have to tolerate a rude or obnoxious lawyer. You are paying his salary, and the attorney needs to know this. In most cases, they do know this and treat their clients with the utmost respect.

Documents Needed to File a Bankruptcy Case

The following are the required documents for filing a bankruptcy case. In many cases, these documents will all be filed by your attorney, but you need to know what these are, how to fill them out, and where they need to be filed. These documents will more than likely be filed via the Internet.

If you are representing yourself, you need to obtain these forms. Your best bet is to go on the United States Courts Web site (**http://www.uscourts.gov/bkforms/**) and download these documents. After completion, you will either have to drive to the courthouse and submit the packet of documents to a clerk or mail them to the courthouse, but the best option would be to go in person. That way, you do not have to worry about it getting lost in the mail or wonder how long it will take until the documents arrive at the court. Once those documents are filed, you will have officially filed for bankruptcy – and all the protections it offers. If you send it through the mail, it could take up to a week for the documents to be received and processed by the clerk. Only then will you have officially filed for bankruptcy.

Unless otherwise noted, these documents are filed whether you file a Chapter 7 or a Chapter 13.

Voluntary Petition

This is a three-page document that may be the most important document when filing your case. If the voluntary petition is not sent, the case cannot be filed. It contains some basic but vital information telling the court it is you who is filing for bankruptcy.

The first part of the first page of the document is just personal information such as you and your spouse's names (if filing jointly), address, and the last four digits of your social security number(s).

Here is what else the form will ask of you:

- How long you have lived in your current location (or district, as it states on the form)

This is to confirm you are available to file in this district. You must have lived in the district in which you are filing bankruptcy for the "better part" of 180 days (6 months). This means that if you moved to Jacksonville, Florida from Cleveland, Ohio just over three months ago, you are eligible to file in Jacksonville. If you moved only two months before, you would not be eligible to file in Jacksonville for another month. You would either have to wait or file for protection in Cleveland.

- Which bankruptcy you are filing (the options on the form are: Chapter 7, 11, 12, or 13)

- Which type of debtor you are (the options are: individual, corporation, or partnership) and whether your debts are mostly consumer or business

For you, it will be individual and consumer debts

- How you will be paying your filing fee (options are: at filing, in installments, or fee waived)

As we discussed, it is extremely rare to get a filing fee waived, though it is exceedingly easy to obtain an installment agreement.

- Estimated number of creditors / amount of debt and value of your property

Do not worry about getting these exactly correct, as you are just estimating

- Whether you have nonexempt assets

- If you are a renter and a landlord has a judgment for eviction against you

- State whether you have a basic understanding of the bankruptcy procedure

- List any prior cases and when and where they were filed

- Indicate whether you have received credit counseling or gotten a waiver

Please read carefully, as you will have to sign in the proper place, your attorney will have to sign, and if you have a non-attorney bankruptcy preparer, they must sign as well.

For your case to be filed, the petition is the only document you need to file at the time of filing the case. Though, each document that needs to be filed after the petition has different deadlines, ranging from 15 to 45 days. The best way to make sure you do not miss a deadline that could result in the dismissal of your case is to file them all at the time of filing the petition.

Here are the other documents that need to be filed shortly after filing the case.

Matrix

The matrix, as it pertains to bankruptcy and not Hollywood, is an important document to file. It is simply a list of your creditors, by and large taken from your credit report. For each creditor, you will need to list their name and full mailing address. Some districts look for account numbers on the matrix as well. To be safe, it would be wise to list the account numbers on the matrix if you know them.

Schedules

The primary function of the schedules is to list your assets, exemptions, income, and expenses.

Schedule A

This would list all your real property. In addition to your home, this will also include any rental properties, timeshares, or vacant lots that you own. You will not list land contracts or leases on this schedule. These are placed on Schedule G.

On the form, you will list the address of the property, the nature of interest in the property, and who owns the property. If the case is jointly filed, you will need to choose "H" if the husband solely owns the property, "W" if the wife solely owns the property, and "J" if the home is jointly owed by the couple. If you live in a state that assigns "community property," you would use "C." Next, you will list the amount of equity you have in the property, and finally, the secured claim, or the amount you currently owe on the mortgage. This figure will also be reported on Schedule D.

If you have no real property, you will simply state "NONE," on the schedule.

Schedule B

This is for all your personal property in your household. Schedule B specifically asks for the value of the following:

- Cash on hand (money on your person or in your home)

- Amounts in bank accounts

- Security deposits with public entities (such as the phone or gas company)

- Household goods (the value of everything in your home)

- Books, pictures, art, collectibles, and memorabilia collections

- Clothes, furs, and jewelry

- Firearms and hobby equipment

- Any insurance policies you have, what type of insurance it is, and, if it is life, whether it is term or whole (A whole life policy means you have the ability to borrow against the policy. If you do not have this provision, it is considered a term policy.)

- Annuities, IRAs, pensions, profit sharing plans, stocks, and bonds

- Interest in any partnerships

- Accounts receivable

- Alimony and child support, which the debtor is entitled to (if you are entitled to receive this but are not receiving, please notate this fact)

- Other liquidated debts owed to the debtor, such as an income tax returns

- Future interests in properties

- Inheritances

- Any patents, licenses, or copy written material

- Customer lists

- Automobiles, trucks, trailers, boats, motorcycles, jet skis, ATVs, or any other motorized vehicle (Do not list leased vehicles here, as there is no secured interest. The debtor does not own the vehicle, instead, they are leasing a vehicle owned by someone else)

- Aircraft and accessories

- Office equipment, furnishings, and supplies

- Machinery

- Inventory

- Animals (farm animals, such as horses and cows, but also any household pets, such as dogs, cats, and birds)

- Crops

- Farming equipment and supplies

There is also a spot for items not fitting into any of the above categories. Just like on Schedule A, if this is a joint case, you will list what the proper ownership is by notating "H," "W," or "J."

Schedule C

Schedule C lists all the exemptions you are claiming in your case. In order for you to properly fill out this schedule, we need to finally discuss exemptions in detail.

Exemptions are designed to help keep those in bankruptcy (and those not in bankruptcy facing garnishments and judgments) from losing everything. Exemptions allow you to protect property up to a certain value. If everything you own fits into the available exemptions, you more often than not have an easy ride in a Chapter 7. If they do not, that is when the trustee will step in to their liquidating role and sell all non-exempt property.

Exemptions play a slightly less important role in a Chapter 13. Even if you have property that is non-exempt, or the value is greater than the allowable exemption, you are allowed to keep your non-exempt property in a Chapter 13. Conversely, debtors are bound to pay back at least the value of the non-exempt property to their creditors. So for example, our friends, the Johnsons from Chapter 3, have figured out that after all their exemptions are used, they have about $14,500 in non-exemptions. The Johnsons will have to pay back at least $14,500 to be split between their unsecured debtors.

The only exception to being allowed to keep exempted property in either bankruptcy chapter is if you refuse to pay your child support or alimony obligations. These are the only types of debts that can come after your exempted property.

Each state has its own exemptions list, and it can be quite lengthy and tricky to find. Many Internet sites that list the state exemptions are incomplete or admittedly only give a fraction of the exemptions available. This is when the bankruptcy process becomes murky for someone with no experience in the law or bankruptcy. This is when you need to seek the advice of an attorney, or, if you are dead set against using an attorney, a non-attorney bankruptcy preparer. They can get the maximum number of exemptions you are entitled to that a Web site may miss or not include.

For a few states, you have two options for exemptions. You may choose the state's exemptions or the federal exemptions. The states that allow you to use either list of exemptions are as follows:

- Arkansas

- Connecticut

- Hawaii

- Massachusetts

- Michigan

- Minnesota

- New Hampshire

- New Jersey

- New Mexico

- Pennsylvania

- Rhode Island

- Texas

- Vermont

- Washington

- Wisconsin

Filers in these states must choose whether they want to take exemptions from one list or the other. They are not allowed to mix and match to use the most beneficial exemption from each list. California does not allow for the federal exemptions, but they have two separate lists of state exemptions; one of which is incredibly similar to the state exemptions.

The Cornell University Law School Web site **(http://www. law.cornell.edu/uscode/html/uscode11/usc_sec_11_ 00000522----000-.html)** lists all of the federal exemptions that you are entitled to if you live in any of the above 15 states. But once again, you may need to seek the advice of an attorney to determine whether the state or federal exemptions are the best for your particular situation.

Some exemptions will exempt an entire item, regardless of the value, while others have exemption limits. Any equity above the exemption is considered non-exempt. Though, many state exemptions and the federal exemptions call for a "wild-card" exemption, which allows anything to be placed there to be exempted up to a certain value. Many times, you are allowed to apply some non-exemptions that could not be exempted because the limit was reached.

Homestead exemptions, which are used on your residence, are a little trickier, and we will discuss these in Chapter 9 of this book.

Now, relating exemptions to Schedule C is simple, as the schedule itself is extremely straightforward. You first check whether you are taking federal (listed as 11 U.S.C. § 522 (b)(2)) or state exemptions (11 U.S.C. § 522 (b)(3)); for most, that is already determined for you, since only state exemptions are available. You will then match your property to the exemption you are entitled to. In the four columns, you will list what property you are exempting, which law is being used for this exemption, how much exemption you are claiming, and the value of the item (not deducting the exemption).

Schedule D

This lists all the secured creditors you have in your case. All secured debts go on here, but remember that lease vehicles are not secured debts and do not belong here (they will go on Schedule G).

In the first column, you will list your entire creditor's address, just like you did on the matrix. The next column will ask you whether there is a co-debtor for this debt. If there is, you will put a check in the column and will want to list these co-debtors on Schedule H. Co-debtors are people who co-signed on a loan with you. They are not a party on the bankruptcy, but they need to be listed. The next box will ask you for the date the debt was incurred, a brief description of the type of debt it is, and the value of the debt. The following three boxes will need to be checked if the debt is "contingent," "unliquidated," or "disputed." The last two columns will ask for the claim and whether there are is an unsecured portion of the debt. If you have no secured debt, check the corresponding box at the top of the form.

Schedule E

This is for priority debts. The first page is more or less a cover page and will ask what kind of priority debt or debts you have. The second page is nearly identical to Schedule D, except you list all your priority debts instead of secured debts. The last column states "amount not entitled to priority, if any," which is the same as when Schedule D asks whether your debt has an unsecured portion. If you have no priority debt, check the corresponding box at the top of the form.

Schedule F

This is for unsecured debts. Again, the form is identical to Schedules D and E, except the unsecured portion box is missing since all these debts are unsecured. If you have no unsecured debt, check the corresponding box at the top of the form.

Schedule G

This is for leases, executory contracts, and land contracts, among others. You will list the full address and a description of the debt, including its ending date. If you have no debts that fit on this schedule, check the corresponding box at the top of the form.

Schedule H

This schedule is for any co-debtors listed in any of the previous schedules. List their full names and their addresses. These creditors must be included on the matrix, unless it is a non-filing spouse who resides in the same household as the debtor.

Schedule I

The listing of your debts and debtors ends with Schedule H. The final two schedules list your current financial situation. Schedule I lists all the income you receive in your household.

The first half of the document will ask about your living situation. You will indicate whether you are "single," "married," "separated," "divorced," or "widowed." You will then be asked to list any dependents you have and their ages. This could be children, step-children, foster children, grandchild, or nieces and nephews whom the debtor has custody of. This could also include an elderly parent or disabled sibling whom the debtor cares for and claims as a dependent on their tax returns. The reason the form asks for ages is because if you have anyone in your household who is over 18, the trustee, judge, and creditors may ask whether that individual contributes income to the household.

The next section will ask for your employer's complete address and for your spouse's, if you have one. Even if you are married but are filing separately, this information needs to be listed. You will also be asked how long you and your spouse have been employed at the current employer(s).

The second half of Schedule I asks you to list all income into your household. If you have a job, it will ask you to list your gross wages and subtract the payroll deductions to come up with a net figure. Then, you will add to this any income received through:

- Running a business

- Having a rental property

- Interests and dividends

- Alimony and child support

- Social security

- Pension

- Any other monthly income (such as family contributions)

You will then add all this income together and come up with your total monthly income.

At the bottom of Schedule I, a question will ask whether you have any reason to believe your income will increase or decrease during the life of your case.

Schedule J

Schedule J lays out the expenses you have in any given month for your household.

The beginning of the page will ask for any rent payments. If you are renting a home, apartment, or condominium, you will put this figure on this line. Some districts let you maintain your mortgage payments in a Chapter 13 case only if you have no arrearages. This means you will be responsible for continuing to pay for your mortgage while you pay the trustee to disperse on all your other debts. If this is the case, you will put your mortgage payment on this line. It will also ask you whether your property taxes and home insurance are included in (or escrowed into) your mortgage payment.

The middle of the form is fairly straightforward, asking you for the amount of your expenses relating to:

- Utilities

- Home maintenance

- Food, clothing, and laundry

- Medical expenses (not for payments on insurance policies)

- Transportation (this is not auto payments; it is for gas, oil changes, auto maintenance, and similar expenses)

- Recreation (including entertainment, subscriptions to newspapers and magazines, and dues for clubs)

- Charity

- Insurance (home, life, health, and auto)

- Taxes (property if not included in mortgage or income if operating your own business that requires money for taxes to be set aside)

- Installment payments (auto, boat, RV, or any other debt leased or purchased and being paid in installments, excluding home mortgages)

- Alimony or child support paid out or to someone not living in your household

- Any business expenses

These are all totaled up and listed at the bottom of Schedule J. This figure is then subtracted from the total income figure that was transferred from Schedule I and included on the line above this one. You then subtract the Schedule J number from the Schedule I number, and you have your monthly net income. In most cases in a Chapter 7, this number will be a negative number, while in a Chapter 13, this has to be a positive number. This is because this number is the figure that will be used as your proposed plan payment. This will be your monthly (or converted to a weekly, bi-weekly, or semi-monthly rate, depending on how you are paid) payment to the trustee.

Declaration of Schedules

This is simply a form you sign stating that all the information contained in the schedules is accurate to the best of your knowledge. Treat this with the utmost importance. If have been found to have knowingly lied or hidden assets on these schedules, you will have perjured yourself and could face prosecution for perjury charges.

Summary of Schedules

You will need to add up all the totals from each Schedule, A through G, and list it in on this page in the proper column.

Statement of Financial Affairs

This is a series of questions asking you about your recent financial history. It is too extensive to describe here, but each question has plenty of directions and notes to help you along. The first two questions (or Sofa #1 and #2) ask you what your income was for the prior two years and how much you have earned in the current calendar year (known as "year-to-date"). Sofa #1 pertains to income from employment or business operation. Sofa #2 refers to any other income, such as child support, rental income, contributions from family members, pension, and social security income, just to name a few.

Certificate of Credit Counseling

As we discussed in Chapter 4, you are required to obtain credit counseling before filing for bankruptcy. Upon completion of the course, you are issued a certificate, which must be filed with the court. Failure to obtain this credit counseling and/or file this certificate could result in the dismissal of your case.

A Form Disclosing Your Social Security Number

The court and the trustee need your social security number for their records. This number will always remain confidential, but you must submit it in a standard form to the clerk. The clerk will then destroy this form or keep it in a secured file and inform the trustee of the number, and the trustee will take the same steps for confidentiality. On every other piece of paperwork, you should only include the last four digits of your social security number.

Other Various Documents

Several various documents need to be filed as well.

- A signed certificate stating you have received notice of your duties, obligations, and rights under the bankruptcy law

- A certificate allowing the bankruptcy to stop any evictions you may be facing

- Disclose any interest you have in an education or individual retirement account

- Chapter 7 Individual Debtor's Statement of Intentions (this is putting in writing what a Chapter 7 debtor is planning to do with their secured property)

- At least 60 days of pay stubs or other income verification for yourself and your spouse, if jointly filed

- Pay stubs or income verification for a non-filing spouse

- At least two years of the most recently filed tax returns

There are two more important documents you need to file: the Plan for a Chapter 13 case and the Means Test for both Chapters. We will discuss those at length in the next chapter.

Both the Means Test and the Plan need to be filed within 15 days of filing the case, so if you have filed all the documents described above, you are in good shape. On the other hand, if you fail to file these additional documents within 15 days, your case could be dismissed.

Make sure you are diligent in having these filed timely.

CHAPTER 6

Filling Out and Understanding The Means Test

"Defeat may test you; it need not stop you. If at first you do not succeed, try another way. For every obstacle, there is a solution. Nothing in the world can take the place of persistence. The greatest mistake is giving up."
– Unknown

In this (lengthy) chapter, we will talk about, digest, and give examples of filling out the Means Test with our made-up friends, the Johnson Family. If you represent yourself in your bankruptcy case, this will be an incredible hurdle for you. This chapter will help you fill this form out, but once again, it would be in your best interests to seek the advice of an attorney.

After filling out this Means Test, you may not get the result you were looking for. If you desired to file a Chapter 7 and are forced to file a Chapter 13 because of the results of the Means Test, then so be it. It may be a disappointment, but if you are committed to making a Chapter 13 case work, it will work for you. As is said in the above quote, do not give up, try your best, and you will succeed.

Things get complicated with the Means Test; this is when

the attorneys earns their money. The Means Test normally plugs in numbers available at the United States Courts government Web site (**http://www.usdoj.gov/ust**) for various allowances. These numbers can be found on this site, but sometimes, a little more insight is needed to properly analyze these numbers and make sure they are correct; please note that these numbers change frequently. Make sure you are using the correct set of numbers for your Means Test based on your filing date.

There are two different types of Means Tests: Form B 22A and Form B 22C. Form B 22A is for Chapter 7 debtors, and Form B 22C is for Chapter 13 debtors. Sometimes, your attorney, trustee, creditors, or judges will call the Means Test by its form number. If one of these parties mentions the Means Test this way, you will know what they are referring to.

If you are consulting a number of books to assist you in the process of bankruptcy, be careful with the other books. The Means Test forms changed in January 2008. If you have books published prior to 2008, they will reflect the old Means Test. While these are still mostly correct, some parts of the Means Test have been changed or amended.

Some of the numbers may be different than your income figures from Schedule I, but that is okay because Schedule I income is your current income, whereas the Means Test is your previous six-month income. So perhaps you were working overtime at your job during the Christmas season, but not now, when you are filing the case in, say, March. You are now making less income than you were six months ago. The overtime would be reflected in your six-month calculation because you had received it during the previous six months. Now that it is April, you no longer get that overtime, so on Schedule I, you would have nothing for overtime. Of course, if you think you will be getting that overtime again next Christmas, you need to make note of the possible change in your income at the bottom of Schedule I. This would also apply if you are making more money now than you were during the previous six-month period.

Do not worry if your numbers on the Means Test and your Schedule I do not match up, as they are actually not supposed to match because most people's income, unless they are salaried, varies.

Let us bring back the family we met in Chapter 3, the Johnsons. They figured out their income for the six-month look-back period. The Means Test is where you use this number.

The Johnsons want to see whether they are eligible to file for a Chapter 7, so they will fill out the Chapter 7 Means Test, Form B 22A, to see whether they qualify. We will show how the Johnsons would fill in the lines of the Means Test as we explain what each line means.

The Chapter 13 form is quite similar to the Chapter 7 form, so we will also refer to the parts that are the same in the Chapter 13 Means Test, or Form B 22C.

Form B 22A (Chapter 7 Means Test) Part I

This section is unique to the Chapter 7 Means Test. Line 1A asks if you are a disabled veteran. If you are, you are required to check a box that declares "under the penalty of perjury" to affirm you are indeed a disabled veteran. Line 1B asks if your debts are not primarily consumer goods; you are once again asked to check a box. Upon checking the box, you can sign the form in Part VIII, and you qualify for a Chapter 7 based on this.

Obviously, this will apply to a tiny portion of people filing bankruptcy, so most of you will continue to the next section.

In our example, although Jim Johnson served in the military, he was never injured, so the Johnsons also move on to Part II.

Form B 22A Part II & Form B 22C (Chapter 13 Means Test) Part I

The first part of this section is different for each Means Test but everything else is similar.

Martial/Filing Status Lines

Line 2 on Form B 22A asks for your marital and filing status. Your options are as follows:

- **Unmarried.** You will complete only Column A – Debtor's income.

- **A married individual filing solo, but currently has separate household from their spouse** (this would be if a spouse has a job in another state and needs to live separately). By checking this box, you affirm once again, under the penalty of perjury, that you maintain separate households. You will complete only Column A.

- **A married individual filing separately, but the couple is living together.** You will need to complete both Column A and Column B – spouse's income.

- **Married couple filing jointly.** You will need to complete both columns.

Line 1 on Form B 22C asks for your marital and filing status; this is more straightforward on this form. It only offers two options: unmarried (complete only Column A) or married (regardless of single or jointly filed, complete both columns).

If a couple is filling jointly, it is customary to install the husband's income in Column A and the wife's income in Column B.

Jim and Judy Johnson are married and filing jointly, so they would check the appropriate box and fill out both columns.

Income (Line 3 in B 22C, Line 2 in B 22A)

The rest of the lines in this section are the same, word for word, in both forms and refer to monthly income. The only difference is the line numbers. Line 3 on B 22A and Line 2 on B 22C asks for gross wages, salaries, tips, bonuses, overtime, and commissions.

From here on, when we discuss the similar sections, we will we list the Chapter 7 Means Test line number first, followed by the Chapter 13 Means Test line number.

We look back at the totals Jim and Judy came up with when figuring out their total income for the past six months. For Mr. Johnson, it was $27,000, and for Mrs. Johnson, it was $12,042. You need to divide this income by six (as in six months) to get your monthly figure. So in this case, Jim Johnson will average $4,500 per month and Judy Johnson will average $2,007 per month.

Business Income (Line 4 or 3)

The next line asks for any income from the operation of a business, profession, or farm. The line has a box with three columns in it – one for gross receipts, one for business expenses, and the last for net business income.

Judy runs her arts and crafts business. She figured out that she had earned $251 in the prior six months. Some months she broke even, some months she gained, and some she lost. Since she figured her income by adding the losses and gains together, she needs to figure out her expenses.

She can do it one of two ways, figure out her actual expenses or just subtract the total from the months when she had a loss from the months when she had a gain.

In November, January, and March, Judy earned a total of $778. In February, she broke even, and in October and December, she lost a total of $527. This is a total net income of $251.

She will need to divide these numbers by six to get the monthly figures. So she will put $129.67 in gross receipts, $87.83 in business expenses, and $41.84 in business income, and carry this over into Column B. Jim does not have business income, so he will leave his column blank or put in a zero.

Rent (Line 5 or 4)

This line is similar to the preceding line. It asks for gross rent; any expenses, such as utilities or other housing maintenance if the debtor or debtors has another property; and net rent income.

Jim's mother resides with the Johnsons and pays $500 per month. The couple does not incur any expenses related to the rented room (this is actually only when someone has a renter in a completely separate property). They did give her a break on her December rent for Christmas, but that is not an expense.

So, they will put $2,500 in for gross receipts, $0 (or nothing) for expenses, and then they will subtract the expenses into the gross, which yields the same – $2,500. Divide it by six, and it will equal $416.67. This number is put in Column A (frequently non-debtor specific information or income that both debtors are entitled to is put into Column A).

Interests, Dividends, and Royalties (Line 6 or 5)

This income could be proceeds from a stock sale, lotto or gambling winnings, and inheritances.

As we stated in Chapter 3, the Johnsons do not have any income that fit in this category.

Pension and Retirement Income (Line 7 or 6)

You would include any income you are receiving from your pension or retirement accounts. Most debtors receiving these forms of income are retired and receiving little to no wages. This line would also be for if you took a 401k (or comparable loan) or cashed your 401k (or comparable account) out when leaving a job.

Again, the Johnsons do not have any income in this category.

Contributions from Other People Not Residing in Household for People in the Household (Line 8 or 7)

This would be for alimony, palimony, or support on children from a previous marriage residing within the household of the new marriage.

Judy is entitled to $650, but rarely gets the exact amount. She listed the amounts sent to her from October through March and got the figure of $1,755. This amount will be put in Column B of this line after being divided by six. This monthly figure is $292.50.

Unemployment (Line 9 or 8)

If you have been unemployed during the prior six-month period, you want to list the total amount you have received over the six-month period and divide it by six.

The Johnsons were not unemployed during this time, so they have no income here.

Income from All Other Sources (Line 10 or 9)

List any income that does not fit in any of the above boxes.

The Johnsons had no other income sources.

Subtotal of Current Monthly Income (Line 11 or 10)

In Form B 22A, this is Line 11, so you will add Lines 3 through 10 for Column A and, if applicable, Column B. In Form B 22C, this is Line 10, so you will add Lines 2 through 9 for Column A and, if applicable, Column B.

Jim Johnson's total for Column A is $4,916.67. Judy Johnson's total for Column B is $2,341.34.

Total Current Monthly Income (Line 12 or 11)

Add the total from Column A to Column B and you have your total current monthly income figure.

For the Johnsons, that total is $7,258.01.

Form B 22A Part III

This is the part on the Chapter 7 Means Test where you will figure out your eligibility for a Chapter 7 case.

Annualized Monthly Income (Line 13)

You will take the figure you got in Line 12 and annualize it, or multiply it by 12, to get your average yearly income figure.

The Johnsons total monthly figure above was $7,258.01. Multiply that figure by 12 and you get $87,096.12.

Applicable Median Family Income (Line 14)

This is where you will compare your state median income level to your own level. As we said, you must obtain this figure (which changes frequently) at **www.usdoj.gov/ust**.

You also must determine how many people are in your household, which can get tricky. Some districts and judges determine the number of people in the household to be the number of dependents on your tax returns plus the debtor or debtors and spouse. Others argue it is anyone in the household, sort of a "heads on beds" approach, meaning the number of people that sleep in the residence on most nights. Once again, seeking the advise of an attorney is paramount.

The median income is determined by which state you live in and how many are in the household. We are going to say that the Johnsons have four in the household. Technically, they have five with Jim's mother, but they do not pay her bills, and she does not contribute to the household other than the rent she pays.

If you are confused, think of it this way: If the Johnsons owned another property, in addition to their residence, and they were renting that house out to a non-family member, they would not include that person as part of the household size. The Johnsons would not pay that renter's bills, and the renter would not contribute to the Johnsons household other than by paying the rent. So if you do not count this person as being in the household, you should not count the mother.

Now on the other hand, if Jim's mom needed healthcare that she could not afford or had other bills the Johnsons paid for, then she would be a dependent and included in this household size number.

Compare this with the figure you have on Line 13, and go to the next line.

Application of Section 707(b)(7) (or Eligibility-Line 15)

You are given two options here, and you must check the box of one of them.

- **The amount on Line 13 is less than or equal to the amount on Line 14.** If this is the case, check the box on the first page of the Means Test that says "The presumption docs not arise," and go directly to Part VIII where you verify and sign. You skip Parts IV, V, VI, and VII. If this is you, congratulations. You have passed the Chapter 7 Means Test and can proceed with filing a Chapter 7 case.

- **The amount on Line 13 is more than the amount on Line 14.** If this is the case, you must complete the entire Means Test. This does not mean you have failed the Means Test just yet. It just requires more information from you to make a determination of your eligibility.

So let us say the Johnsons live in Florida. As we discussed above, they are a household of four. The median income for a household of four in the state of Florida is $64,280. Their amount on Line 13 is $87,096.12. The amount on Line 13 is more than the amount on Line 14, so the Johnsons need to continue on with the Means Test.

To get another perspective, let us say that Jim and Judy live in the state that has the highest median income: Connecticut. For a household of four, the median income is $95,183. This would put the Johnsons' Line 13 number at less than the Line 14 number. So if the Johnsons were lucky enough to live in Connecticut and wanted to file a Chapter 7, they would be quite happy today.

Sadly for the Johnsons, they are Floridians, and as such, they must continue on with the Means Test.

Form B 22C Part II & III

Before we continue on with the Chapter 7 Means Test, we need to talk about the unique parts of the Chapter 13 Means Test. Part II is where you determine your commitment period. It is different than the Chapter 7 form, which necessitates its own section to describe it.

As we have discussed, you do not need to pass the Means Test to file for a Chapter 13, but whether you pass it determines how long you will be locked into the bankruptcy.

The first line of Part II, Line 12, simply asks you to enter the amount from Line 11. If we are still using the Johnsons as an example, their Line 11 figure was $7,258.01.

Marital Adjustment (Lines 13 and 14)

This applies only to single-filing debtors with a non-filing spouse. This would be the equivalent of the option on Line 2 of the Chapter 7 Means Test, or Form B 22A, which asks whether a debtor and their non-filing spouse are maintaining separate residences.

If this applies to your case, you must list the basis for excluding this income listed in Part I of the B 22C, which specific income (if you are excluding only part of the spouse's income), and how much of that income you are excluding. If this does not apply to you, then leave the line blank or write zero. Rewrite the number from Line 11 (and Line 12) on Line 14.

If this does apply to you, on Line 13, total up the income that you have excluded, subtract it from Line 12, and enter the result in the column on Line 14.

This does not apply to our example family, the Johnsons.

Annualized Monthly Income (Line 15)

This is the same as Line 13 on the Chapter 7 Means Test. Multiply the number from Line 14 by 12, and you have your average yearly income.

Applicable Median Family Income (Line 16)

In the Chapter 7 Means Test, we saw that the Johnsons did not pass the first part of the Means Test and had to continue to seek their eligibility for a Chapter 7. If Jim and Judy desired to file a Chapter 13, this part would determine how long they would be in the bankruptcy.

It does not matter what type of bankruptcy you file, the numbers are all the same. So if we stick with the notion that the Johnsons live in Florida, and their household size is four, then their median income is $64,280, the same as in a Chapter 7.

Application of § 1325(b)(4) (or Length of Commitment Period-Line 17)

The options here are:

- **The amount on Line 15 is less than the amount on Line 16.** If this is true, you check the box on this line and check the box on page 1 stating "The applicable commitment period is 3 years," and continue to Part III." This does not limit you to only three years in the bankruptcy; if you have large debts that may need longer to be paid off, you can propose a longer plan. It just means you can propose a three-year (or 36-month) Plan.

- **The amount on Line 15 is not less than the amount on Line 16.** If this applies to you, check the box on this line and check the box on page 1 stating "The applicable commitment period is five years," and continue to Part III. This means you cannot propose any plan that does not last five years. Be aware that it cannot last longer than five years because bankruptcies are not allowed to exceed five years (or 60 months).

There is one exception to a case that is over the median income being allowed to run less than five years. That is if the debtor or debtors have enough excess income to pay back their unsecured creditors at least 100 percent of what they owe (sometimes on 100 percent cases, if the debtor can do it, the trustee or creditor will ask for interest of up to 7 percent). Cases like this can propose a three- or four-year (or 36- or 48-month) Plan.

So by using the figures and logic from the Chapter 7 annualized income section, the Johnsons, if they lived in Florida, would be required to stay in the bankruptcy for five years. If, on the other hand, they lived in Connecticut, they would only be locked in for three years.

The first line, Line 18, of Part III again asks for the amount that was in Line 11. Once again, we will use the Johnsons figure of $7,258.01.

Marital Adjustment (Line 19 and 20)

No, this is not a typo. On the Chapter 13 Means Test, Form B 22C, there are two lines titled "Marital Adjustment." Like the other one, this applies to single-filers who are married and maintaining separate households. This one is used for people who did not exclude any income on the Marital Adjustment on Line 13. Do not try to use both lines. The purpose of this second Marital Adjustment is to explain why the disposable income should be less; we will get to the disposable income soon. It is filled out the same way as the previous Marital Adjustment. If this does not pertain to you, write zero or leave it blank.

Line 20 asks you to subtract the number listed in Line 19 from the number in Line 18 (which was the number from 11). For most, the number in Line 19 will be zero, and you will get the same number. In the Johnsons' case, the number is $7,258.01.

Annualized Current Monthly Income (Line 21)

This asks you to multiply the number from Line 20 by 12. Once again for Jim and Judy Johnson, it will be $87,096.12.

Applicable Median Family Income (Line 22)

It once again asks you for this amount, which is listed on Line 16. Remembering that figure of $64,280, you once again compare it to your annualized monthly income.

Application of § 1325(b)(3)(Line 23)

The options here are:

- **The amount on Line 21 is more than the amount of Line 22.** If this is the case, check the box here and on page 1 stating, "Disposable income is determined under § 1325(b)(3)," and continue with the Means Test. This means you are bound to pay back what you determine as your disposable income at the end of the Means Test.

- **The amount on Line 21 is not more than the**

amount on Line 22. If this applies to you, check the box here and the box saying, "Disposable income is not determined under § 1325(b)(3)" on page 1. You can also skip the rest of the sections until you get to Part VII, which is just you affirming and signing. This means you are bound to pay back only what your excess income from Schedule J will allow.

Move on to Part IV of Form B 22 C.

Form B 22A Part IV

We now come back to the Chapter 7 Means Test, which is somewhat unique from the Chapter 13 Means Test. This Part is quite similar to the Parts we just described in Parts III and IV of the Chapter 13 Means Test (Form B 22C), but is important enough to warrant its own section.

The first line, Line 16, in this Part simply asks for the amount from Line 12, which was $7,258.

Marital Adjustment (Line 17 and 18)

Whereas the Chapter 13 Means Test has two, this is the only Marital Adjustment on the Chapter 7 Means Test. It refers back to the Line in Part II of this form. Treat it the same way as described in the sections above on the Chapter 13 Marital Adjustments. Then, in Line 18, subtract Line 17 from Line 16. Again, for most people, the Marital Adjustment will be zero, and the same number will appear on Lines 16 and 18.

Move on to Part V of Form B 22A.

Form B 22A Part V & Form B 22C Part IV

These Parts are identical to each other. They relate to the calculations of deductions for income. Since they are similar, we will cover them both together.

Many of these items are for allowances at a pre-set amount in which you may be entitled to. Again, you must consult the United States Courts Web site like you have done for many other factors – most recently, the average median income for your household.

So while we will continue to use our example family, the Johnsons, it is impossible to advise you of the exact amount of allowances you are entitled to, if any.

The purpose of this section of the Means Test is to determine the expenses that you incur in an average month. This will be subtracted from your income to determine how much you can pay back to your unsecured creditors.

Once again, we will go line by line listing the Chapter 7 Means Test (Form B 22A) first, and then the Chapter 13 Means Test (Form C 22C).

National Standards: Food, Clothing, and Other Items (Line 19A or 24A)

This is a national number based on the amount of people in your household.

Factoring in the four people in their household, the Johnsons' allowance for this line is $1,370.

National Standards: Healthcare (Line 19B or Line 24B)

This is the new kid on the block. Earlier in this chapter, we told you that the Means Test forms have recently been changed., and this is one of the major changes in the new forms. This has a mini-worksheet to determine your healthcare deduction allowance. The old format had you insert your actual healthcare expense, while the new format figures an allowance for each member of the family.

This may be good for some people because it will increase the amount they are able to deduct now, as opposed to the Means Test forms from 2005 through 2007. On the other hand, for others, it may decrease the amount they can claim as an expense if they have a sick child or an elderly parent in their care.

The worksheet is broken into two parts. One is for members in the household under 65 years of age and the other is for household members who are 65 and over. The under 65 individuals receive a $54 per month deduction, while their older relatives get a $144 per month deduction.

You will enter this number in a1. for under 65 years and a2. for 65 and over. Next, you will list the number of people fitting in this category in b1. and b2. Finally, you will come up with a subtotal for each category.

Jim, Judy, and (of course) their two children are all under 65 years old. Their allowance is $54 each, so that would be put in a1. There are four members at that designation, so $54 (allowance) X 4 (members of household) = $216.

We have said that despite Jim's mother living in the

household, she does not count as an official member, since she pays rent but pays all her own expenses. If she did count as an official household member, her allowance is $144. That figure, $144 (allowance) X 1 (member of household) = $144. We would then add that to the $216 from the members of the household under 65, but as we said, Jim's mom is not included, so the total for this line is $216.

Local Standards: Housing and Utilities; Non-Mortgage Expenses (Line 20A and 25A)

This is for your non-mortgage home expenses. You will have to search under your home state and locate your county in the list to figure out your allowance. Once again, another factor in this figure is the household size.

Since we know Jim and Judy Johnson live in Florida, we will look at the United States Court's Web site, **www.usdoj. gov/ust**, and look for the state of Florida. Let us say the Johnsons live in Lakeland, Florida, which is located in Polk County. Their allowance for non-mortgage expenses is $510.

Do not close out of this Web page just yet, as you will need it for the next line.

Local Standards: Housing and Utilities: Mortgage/Rent Expense (Line 20B and 25B)

This is the figure right next to the one you just looked up. You will plug it into the mini-worksheet listed on this line. In the top box (a.), you will list the allowance, on the second box (b.), you will list your mortgage payment, and finally (c.), you will list the net result. Do not worry if you have a negative number, because you will in most cases. If this is the case, do not list a negative number in the right column. Either list $0 or leave it blank.

The Johnsons notice their housing expense for Polk County is $790 and their mortgage payment is $1,200.

They list this as follows:

    a. $ 790   (allowance)

    b. $1,200   (mortgage payment)

    c. $ 410   (net)

Let us do the calculation for if the Johnsons lived in St. Augustine, Florida in the county of St. John's. St. John's County is one of the highest-income counties in the country, and as such, has a higher allowance. More than likely, if the Johnsons lived in this area, their mortgage payment would be higher, but for this case, let us just say it is still $1,200. The allowance for a household of four in this county is $1,290.

    a. $1,290

    b. $1,200

    c. $ 90

So if the Johnsons lived in St. John's County, they could claim $90 of their allowance and move that over to the column on the right. As we said, it is more likely you will have a negative number and list a zero in the right column.

Local Standards: Housing and Utilities Adjustment (Line 21 or 26)

If you feel you should be allowed additional expenses or allowances not afforded in the above line, list those here. It is rare to include anything here, and if you do, it will be deeply scrutinized by the trustee and your creditors. This is another case of when an attorney would help you decide whether filling out this line if an option for you.

Local Standards: Transportation (Line 22A or 27A)

The other major change in the Means Test relates to transportation. The next four lines address car ownership and transportation costs. Again, these allowances are determined by where you live. With this new streamlined version, a national standard for non-vehicle ownership or public transportation costs has been set. This increases for some, but also decreases significantly for others. New York City has an extensive public transportation system and the congestion of the area, precludes some from owning a vehicle. Under the old figures, a car-less New Yorker was allowed $313 for public transportation. With the implementation of the new system, this number has been slashed by half to $163.

This line will ask you how many vehicles you own. Your options are zero, one, or two or more. Even if you select zero, you get an allowance, which as we discussed above, is $163.

Rather than searching for these figures by state like with the others, you search through regions. You will choose from Northeast, Midwest, South, and West. Each region will list several metropolitan areas within these regions. If your city is not listed, you will just use the regional figures.

The Johnsons live in the South Region, but the only Florida city in the list that is close to where they live is Miami, almost 200 miles away from Lakeland. Obviously, they would not use the Miami figures; they will use the regional figures.

The Johnsons have two cars because both Jim and Judy need transportation to and from work; most working Americans have two cars, so this is a common occurrence. They would be allowed to claim a $362 allowance for having two vehicles. If they only had one car, they would be allowed $181.

Local Standards: Additional Public Transportation Expense (Line 22B or 27B)

This is for people who perhaps own a vehicle or vehicles, but also use public transportation. This could mean that you take the subway, train, or bus to work, and maybe you drive to the station or depot and do a "park and ride." If this applies to you, you may use the public transportation figure from above.

Local Standards: Ownership/Lease Expense: Vehicle 1 (Line 23 or 28) & Vehicle 2 (Line 24 or 29)

The next two lines are the same. The first asks you for information about your first car, and the second line asks you for information on your second car, if you have one. If you have no vehicles, leave these two lines blank. If you have only one vehicle, fill in the first line and leave the second line blank.

This is based on a national figure instead of a regional figure. You get $478 each for two vehicles but if you have more than two vehicles, you are out of luck. The allowance only applies to the first two vehicles. That means you get $478 if you have one vehicle and $478 if you have a second vehicle. If you have more than two, you cannot claim another allowance.

Again, these lines are set up with a box. The first part (a.) asks for the IRS Transportation Standard, which is the $478. The next part (b.) will ask you for your monthly car or lease payment, and the last part (c.) will ask you for the net income.

Jim drives a lease car and his payment is $285 per month. Judy drives an SUV, which the family purchased a few years back, and her payment is $344. So the Johnsons have figured their ownership expenses as follows:

a. $478 (standard)

b. $285 (payment)

c. $193 (net)

So they will put the net figure in the right column, move onto the next line, and do the exact same type of calculation for vehicle number two.

a. $478 (standard)

b. $344 (payment)

c. $134 (net)

Again, the Johnsons will put the net figure of $134 in the right column.

Taxes (Line 25 & Line 30)

At last, we get to install some of your real expense figures instead of using the national, state, or regional allowances. This is for any federal, state, and local taxes that have been taken out of your paycheck or that you are required to pay as a business owner or from being self-employed. This figure many not necessarily be the exact amount of taxes taken out of your paycheck each pay period.

If you have Microsoft Excel and know a little bit about how to use it, you may be able to use the calculation used by Krispen Carroll's office, one of the Chapter 13 trustee's offices in Detroit, to verify this line when doing a case review.

You will first want to obtain a gross figure. For this, you will want to look at the income you have listed on Schedule I and multiply it by 12. Next, you will figure out your federal tax percentage by dividing the total taxes into the total income from your most recent tax return; these are lines 62 and 22 on the tax returns, respectively. The trustee's office then estimated the total state tax as 4.40 percent, social security at 6.20 percent, and Medicare at 1.45 percent. The trustee estimates this at a conservatively high figure. If you work in a city that deducts payroll taxes, you need to take this into account. On average, city taxes are only about 1.5 percent, but you should check your pay stub or ask your payroll department to be sure.

The Johnsons do this calculation:

They figure out their yearly income to be $87,096. Next, they figure their tax rate on their most recently filed returns and they put that in the tax percentage field; their percentage is 8.98 percent. Notice how all the figures below change, while the percentages stay the same. The Johnsons do not have city taxes, so they can arrive at their total tax of $1,526.26, which is calculated with the Excel program by the formulas inserted. They record this figure and move to the next line. Below is the worksheet the Johnsons used, and you can model your calculation off of it as well.

Johnson's Worksheet			
Gross	**$ 87096**	(Total gross from Schedule I multiplied by 12)	
Federal Tax	**8.98%**	$ 7,821.22	Divided Debtor's tax (Line 62) by total income (Line 22) from most recent ITRT
State Tax	4.40%	$ 3,832.22	Trustee's estimate is without deductions; therefore conservatively high
FICA	6.20%	$ 5,399.95	Trustee's estimate is not capped based on income; therefore conservatively high
Medicare	1.45%	$ 1,262.89	Trustee's estimate is not capped based on income; therefore conservatively high
No City Tax	0.00%	$ -	<--Keep this as is if the Debtor does not pay city payroll taxes
City Tax	**1.50%**		**$ 1,306.44** <-- Copy this number to the left if the debtor works in a city which
	Total Tax:	$ 18,316.29	Payment of city taxes
Total tax to appear on MT Line 30:	$ 1,526.36		

Involuntary Employment Deductions (Line 26 or 31)

You will list any deductions out of your paycheck for union dues, mandatory retirement deductions, uniform costs, parking, or any other necessary employment fees. Do not include voluntary deductions, such as 401k contributions.

Judy must pay for her uniforms to be cleaned at work. The cost is minimal, at $2 per week. She also gets $30 taken out for union dues per month. These deductions do not come out of every check; instead, they are deducted on the first check of the month. Judy must figure out how much comes out for uniform cleaning each month. She figures if they take out $2 per week and there are 52 weeks in a year, $104 is taken out every year. She then divides this figure by 12 to get her monthly figure, which is $8.67 per month. Add this to the once monthly union dues, and the Johnsons have $38.67 coming out each month in involuntary deductions. They list this figure in the right column.

Life Insurance (Line 27 or 32)

You will list any monthly fees for life insurance policies.

The Johnsons have policies on themselves and their children, and they cost a total of $100 per month.

Court Ordered Payments (Line 28 or 33)

This is for any child support or alimony you must pay monthly.

Education for Employment or for Care of a Physically or Mentally Challenged Child (Line 29 or 34)

This would be the cost of education for a child if they have limitations that prevent attending a regular school.

Childcare (Line 30 or 35)

Anyone who has children in daycare knows the financial pinch involved. Enter the amount you spend on childcare or after school programs.

The Johnsons are lucky that Jim's mother lives with them. She watches the three-year-old three days a week and the ten-year-old after school until Jim and Judy arrive home from work, so their child care costs are minimal. Even with only using daycare two days per week, it still costs the family $100 per week.

Healthcare (Line 31 or 36)

List the amount you actually spend on healthcare. This does not include the amount you pay or that is deducted from your check for health insurance. You will list these amounts later.

The Johnsons are lucky to have good insurance, which requires only $10 to be paid for each doctor visit and prescription that is filled. The family figures that, on average, they spend $80 on healthcare.

Telecommunications (Line 32 or 37)

This is for amenities above and beyond the usual, such as home phone service and basic cell phone coverage. This could include but is not limited to call waiting, caller identification, special long distance, or Internet. If this number is large, the trustee can question the need for some of these expenses, so be prepared to provide good reason for keeping your elaborate cell phone plans and other lavish items.

The Johnsons figure they spent about $100 on these types of items. Trustees will rarely raise an eyebrow about $100 being listed here.

Total Expenses from Lines 19-23 or 24-27 (Line 33 or 38)

The Johnsons add all their expenses and come up with $4,629.43.

You then move on to the next section, which asks about more expenses.

Health Insurance, Disability Insurance, and Health Savings Account Expenses (Line 34 or 39)

This is broken down into three sections, and you are asked to list each different health insurance type here. Health insurance on a., disability insurance on b., and health savings accounts on c., and then add these figures together and list in the right column.

The insurance all comes out of Jim's paycheck, as Judy receives increased pay for opting out of her company's benefits package.

The family has $575 taken out each month for health insurance, $200 each month for disability, and nothing for the health savings account for a total of $775.

Contributions to the Care of Household or Family Members (Line 35 or 40)

This would be for care of an elderly parent, sibling, or any other members of the family who have no means to care for themselves. This could relate to a person living in your house or outside your home.

The Johnsons do not provide care for Jim's mother, so they leave this blank.

Protection Against Family Violence (Line 36 or 41)

This line is for any expenses incurred to protect your family under the Family Violence Prevention and Services Act.

Home Energy Costs (Line 37 or 42)

If you feel you are entitled to additional costs for providing power to your home, enter the amount here, but be ready to provide documentation to the trustee to back up this claim.

Education for Children 18 and Under (Line 38 or 41)

This would apply to any payments for a private school for children. This does not apply to college courses. You cannot exceed $137.50 per child. As in the prior case, be ready to provide documentation for this expense.

The Johnsons' school-aged child attends public school, which requires no tuition.

Additional Food and Clothing Expense (Line 39 or 44)

If you feel you are entitled to additional food and clothing expenses, you can enter an amount in this line. This cannot be more than 5 percent of the combined food and clothing allowances allowed in Line 19A or 24A.

Once again, the trustee may request documentation.

Continued Charitable Contribution (Line 40 or 45)

This would be any charity you currently donate to.

The Johnsons used to donate more to charity, but have cut back in recent months leading up to the bankruptcy, although they still give $10 per week at their church. By using the weekly to monthly calculation we did for Line 26 or 31, we come up with $43.33 per month.

Total Additional Expense Deductions from Lines 34-40 or 39-45 (Line 41 or 46)

The Johnsons' total for this section is $618.33

Future Payments on Secured Claims (Line 42 or 47)

This is for all your secured payments for the next 60 months, or five years. Remember, a leased vehicle is not secured, so you will not list these payments here.

Once again, you are required to fill out a series of boxes. You will give the name of the creditor in the first column, a description of the secured claim in the next column, and average monthly payment amount in the third column. The fourth column asks whether this payment includes taxes or insurance. Obviously, this will only apply if the secured debt is a mortgage. The box has three entries, but if you have more than three creditors, continue on a separate sheet of paper with entry number four.

Here are the most common types of debts you will list here:

- Ongoing mortgage payments (not arrears)

- Property tax

- Water bills

- Vehicle purchases (not leases)

Even if you have "surrendered" (or allowed the property to be reclaimed by the creditor) a piece of property prior to or in the early stages of your bankruptcy, you still need to list that property here.

To get the average monthly payment, you will need to divide the total contractual amount still owed by 60, representing the 60 months you are required to be in a Chapter 13 (you also do this for a Chapter 7 Means Test). If it is a continuing debt, such as a mortgage, do not worry about dividing the actual contractual rate, as that is most likely several hundreds of thousands of dollars. Instead, use the actual mortgage payment you pay each month.

The Johnsons list their secured debts as follows. Remember that for everything but continuing claims, you must divide the contractual amount still owed by 60:

Name of Creditor	Property	Avg. Mo. Pmt.	Include Txs & Ins?
a. Countrywide	1234 Any St.	$1200	Yes
b. Ford Motor Co	'05 Explorer	$ 344	N/A
c. Polk County Water	1234 Any St.	$ 189	N/A

If the Johnsons had more secured debts, they would continue on another sheet, but they only have three secured debts and can move on. Remember, we said the family had two vehicles, one a purchase and one a lease. Notice that we listed only the purchased vehicle.

Thcy thcn add up all thc monthly payments in the third column and record the figure in the right column. That figure is $1,733.

Other Payments on Secured Properties (Line 43 or 48)

This line is mainly for arrears of secured claims. If you have arrears on your home, you will divide the total arrears amount by 60 and list here. The box on the line is just about the same as the line preceding it, except the taxes and insurance box has been removed.

Jim and Judy have a $4,500 arrearage on their home. Divided by 60, that amount is $75. The Ford Motor Company debt is non-continuing and, as such, has no arrears. So the only thing in this line for the Johnsons is $75. That number is moved to the right column.

Payments of Pre-petition Priority Claims (Line 44 or 49)

We discussed priority claims in Chapter 3. They are primarily IRS and state unpaid taxes and support obligations. The total debts of all your priority claims will be divided by 60.

The Johnsons have a small unpaid IRS debt for unpaid taxes on Judy's business; the IRS amount is $267. They do not owe any child support or other priority debts, so their total priority amount if $267. Divided by 60, this number is $4.45.

Chapter 13 Administrative Expenses (Line 45 or 50)

This needs to be completed in both Means Tests. It gives you a rough estimate of what the administrative expenses will be for trustee fees. You will list your projected Chapter 13 Plan payment, which is found on Schedule J. You then list the current multiplier for your district. Once again, that figure is found on the United States Court's Web site.

After doing the multiplication calculation, the Johnsons put $20.07 in the right column.

Total Deductions for Debt Payment Lines 42-45 or 47-50 (Line 46 or 51)

The Johnsons came up with $1,832.45 for their number.

Total of ALL Deductions for Lines 33, 41 & 46 or 38, 46 & 51 (Line 47 or 52)

The Johnsons add all these lines together and come up with $7,071.21.

Form B 22 A, Part VI: Determination of § 707 (b)(2) Presumption

This is where the Means Test forms part company momentarily. Each one has its own determination in this section, which is one of the final sections.

Line 48 asks for you to reenter the amount from Line 18. Line 49 asks you to reenter the amount from Line 47 and Line 50 asks you to subtract Line 49 from 48 and record the result in the right column. Then Line 51 asks you to multiply this result by 60.

Here is how Jim and Judy filled out this part:

Line 48 (figure from Line 18)	$ 7,258
Line 49 (figure from Line 47)	$ 7,071.21
Line 50 (Line 48 minus Line 49)	$ 186.79
Line 51 (Multiply Line 50 by 60)	$11,207.40

Initial Presumption Determination (Line 52)

You are given the following three options:

- **The amount of Line 51 is less than $6,575.** If this is you, you will check the box stating "The presumption does not arise" on the top of page 1 and skip down to the verification in Part VIII. You have passed the Means Test and can file for a Chapter 7.

- **The amount set forth on Line 51 is more than $10,950.** Check the box on page 1 stating "The presumption arises." Complete Part VII if necessary and VIII for signature. Unfortunately, you cannot file for a Chapter 7 and must file for a Chapter 13.

- **The amount on Line 51 is at least $6,575, but not more than $10,950.** Complete the remainder of this section.

The Johnsons expected to have to file for a Chapter 13, so filling out the Chapter 7 Means Test was a formality. As you see, they did not pass the Means Test and were unable to qualify for a Chapter 7 case, but instead, they will file for a Chapter 13 case. The good news for the Johnsons is that they can install close to, if not all of, the information from the Chapter 7 Means Test into the Chapter 13 Test easily, because as we have seen, the two forms are incredibly similar.

Enter the Amount of Your Total Non-priority Unsecured Debt (Lines 53-54)

If you checked the third option on Line 52, you will go on to Line 53. Simply enter the amount of unsecured debts you have and then multiply this number by 0.25 in Line 54.

Secondary Presumption Determination (Line 55)

Two options here:

- **The amount on Line 51 is less than the amount on Line 54.** If this is you, you will check the box on page 1, "The Presumption does not arise," and you can file for Chapter 7.

- **The amount on Line 51 is equal to or bigger than the amount on Line 54.** Check the box on page 1 for "The Presumption arises," and complete Part VII, if necessary, and VIII for verification. You will have to file for a Chapter 13.

As we have discussed previously, you can argue that an exception should be made for you if you are ineligible for a Chapter 7, but this is difficult.

Form B 22C-Part V Determination of Disposable Income

Now we will tackle the unique section of the Chapter 13 Means Test. The first line in this section, Line 53, will ask you to reenter the amount from Line 20.

The Johnsons use their Chapter 7 figures in this section, and Line 20 corresponds to Line 12 on Form B 22A. They record this figure, $7,258.01, on Line 53 of Form B 22C. The next line asks you to list any support income. Remember we said Judy is entitled to support for her first born, but gets only a fraction of it. This amount was reported on Line 8 of the Chapter 7 Means Test when the Johnsons filled it out and Line 7 of the Chapter 13 Means Test when they completed that after finding out they were ineligible for a Chapter 7. This figure is $292.50.

Qualified Retirement Deductions (Line 55)

You will list any retirement, 401k, 403b savings plans, or repayments here.

The Johnsons both contribute to a 401k, and Jim has a 401k loan. The total deducted out of both of their checks weekly is $150.

Line 56 asks you to rewrite the number from Line 52, which for the Johnsons was $7,071.21

Deductions for Special Circumstances (Line 57)

If you feel you are entitled to other deductions not mentioned anywhere in the Means Test, list these here. Be prepared to provide detailed reasoning and documentation.

The Johnsons leave this blank.

The next line, Line 58, will once again ask you to add up a number of lines. In this case, it is Lines 54, 55, 56, and 57, and the Johnsons result is $7,513.71. The following line, Line 59, will ask you to subtract Line 58 from Line 53. The result for the Johnsons is a negative number, -$255.70.

Do not panic if you have a negative figure like the Johnsons, as this is actually fairly common. That means that theoretically, you can pay back nothing to your creditors, but other factors go into determining this, such as your disposable income, so this may not always be the case.

Let us say that the Johnsons did have a positive number and a large positive number at that. Let us give the Johnsons the arbitrary amount of $1,280 for the disposable income on Line 59. If they multiply this by 60, for the 60-month plan, the result is $76,800.60. That means in the course of a 60-month plan, the Johnsons can pay back a total of nearly $77,000 to their unsecured creditors. Unless they have many unsecured creditors, they more than likely will be required to pay back 100 percent of their debts. If their unsecured debts were, say $100,000, they would be required to pay back 77 percent. We get this figure by dividing $76,800.60 into $100,000 and get 0.768006, or 77 percent. This is not required to be done on the Means Test by the trustee, as he or she will normally go ahead and do this calculation; it may be a sticking point in the Confirmation process if you do not agree to remit this to your creditors.

Form B 22A-Part VII-VIII, Form B 22C-Part VI-VII Additional Expense Claims

On both Means Tests, if you feel you are entitled to other expenses, you can list them here. This section is rarely completed.

The last section is just for a signature, and again, is under the penalty of perjury. If it is proven you have knowingly lied while filling out this form, perjury charges could be sought.

At last, the Means Test chapter comes to a close. As you can see, since we discussed in such vast length, it is extremely complicated. That is why it is so important you seek out an attorney.

We will next move on to the final document needed for bankruptcy. This applies to Chapter 13 cases only. If you have determined you are eligible for a Chapter 7, you can skip the first part of the next chapter regarding the Chapter 13 Plan.

We will also discuss proof of claims in the next chapter, so if you are filing a Chapter 7, you should read the second half of the next chapter.

Chapter 13 Plan and Proof of Claims

"Always have a plan, and believe in it. Nothing happens by accident."
– *Chuck Knox, Football Coach*

Perhaps Coach Knox, former coach of the National Football League's Los Angeles Rams, did not realize his words would be used outside of the gridiron. His words can be applied directly to the bankruptcy world. Yes, we have discussed the Plan in a Chapter 13 briefly, and will get to it shortly, but the word "plan" in the quote can apply to anyone filing for bankruptcy, whether you are filing for Chapter 7 or 13.

You need to go into this process with a clear idea – or plan. If you make a plan to file bankruptcy and you stick to it, for a few months in a Chapter 7 or a few years in a Chapter 13, then you will be much better off in the long run. Eventually your credit will get better, and you will be free to buy the things you need and desire with your new found restraint and buyers savvy that has been achieved through this process.

Now that you have mastered the Means Test, it is on to the Plan. To follow your "plan," you have to file your Plan (for Chapter 13 filers only). As was stated in the last few chapters, it is especially important to file this as soon as possible to avoid any potential problems in your case, such as a dismissal.

The Chapter 13 Plan

This is essentially the basis of your entire Chapter 13 bankruptcy case. This document tells the court, trustee, and creditors what you plan to pay to the trustee to be disbursed to your creditors, how much you plan to pay your creditors, and how long your case will last.

It is impossible to describe exactly what type of plan you will file. Each bankruptcy district across the country has its own type of plan conforming to local bankruptcy rules, but the basics of the plan are universal, and we will list those below.

Commitment Period and Plan Term

You will need to remember the commitment period from your Means Test when beginning to fill out your Plan because you will list that on here as well. If your monthly income was less than your state median income, then your commitment period is three years. If your monthly income was more than the state median income, your commitment period is five years.

If you are committed to five years, and are able to propose a 100 percent plan to your unsecured creditors, then you can be out of the bankruptcy in three years, but this is the only exception.

On the other hand, if you are committed to only three years, you can propose either a three-, four-, or five-year plan. The benefit of having a longer case even though you are only required to be in for three years is that your payment will be less, and larger debts have the opportunity of being paid off during the bankruptcy, as opposed to surviving the discharge. The disadvantage is that you are constrained by your bankruptcy for five long years.

Plan Payment

This is based on how often you are paid and can be proposed as:

- Monthly (self-employed, business owners, and retirement and pension recipients would propose this frequently)

- Semi-monthly (for those who are employed and paid twice per month)

- Bi-weekly (for those who are employed and paid every other week, or unemployment recipients who get benefits in this frequency) or weekly (for most who are paid hourly or are in retail).

The frequency of the payment is the monthly excess income from your Schedule J, converted to the proper frequency. This is how much you will pay to the trustee for the next three to five years, who will then disburse to your creditors.

Income Tax Refunds

In some districts, your income tax refund is sent directly

to the trustee; in others, you will be asked whether you will be contributing your income tax refund to the trustee on your Plan form. Most times, this is not an option; you must relinquish any tax refunds you will receive for the next three to five years. This is because a tax refund is considered an "asset of the estate," or as income.

This is a bankruptcy-related bummer for two reasons. Sometimes, you look forward to that refund every year and while in a Chapter 13, this is taken from you. Second, even if you received a sizeable refund, which was then handed over to the trustee, it does not mean your case will be complete sooner than originally planned.

In some cases, if you propose a 100 percent payment to your creditors, you will be allowed to keep your income tax refunds. Since the bankruptcy reforms have come about, this is the only exception.

If you are a person who pays a little more through the year so that you can get a nice bonus of a sizeable tax refund in the spring or early summer, you may want to rethink your logic. By overpaying your taxes throughout the year, you are losing the ability to have that income throughout the year. In most cases, you will get much less back in a tax refund than you would have received from a year of decreased deductions. Either way, any refund will be doled up between your creditors just like a bankruptcy payment would be.

Sometimes you can show the court exigent circumstances to retain your income tax refund. This would be allowed if you showed the court that an emergency had come up that required the money to be used to pay for this emergency.

Perhaps you need a new roof, hot water heater, or other necessary appliances in your home. Obviously, you cannot live your life without these types of appliances, and you would need to address the situation appropriately. In many cases, the court would rather have you keep your income tax refund so that you will not miss any plan payments; missing plan payments could derail your case. Please note, though, you had better have plenty of documentation of your troubles for the court to grant such a motion.

Bonuses and profit sharing all fall under this income tax refund umbrella. Almost all forms of income are considered property of the estate.

Order of Payments / Descriptions of Debts

When your creditors are paid is one of those items that vary from district to district.

The trustee will always be paid first. They get paid anywhere from 4 to 10 percent of what they disburse; their percentage can fluctuate at some points in the year. They are not allowed to make a profit, but also cannot go in to the red, so they may adjust their trustee percentage based on their office budget. If the total for their yearly office budget is getting near, they will reduce their fee. If they feel they need to increase their fee to meet their budget, they will do that as well. In rare cases, the trustee may hit their budget late in their fiscal year, and then for the last few months of that year, the trustee will take no fees.

Some districts let you pay your filing fee within the plan, and that is paid just after the trustee fee. In most districts, the attorney's fees are paid next.

From there, it is unclear. Some districts pay your mortgage before any other debt, and for others, child support arrears are paid first. Either way, secured claims and priority claims are paid in whichever way the local rules state. Finally, in all cases, unsecured claims are paid last.

In addition to listing how they will be paid in the Plan, you must list the creditor's name, amount of the debt, and how long you are proposing to pay off this debt, as you may want to pay off a debt prior to the case being discharged. You will only list the secured, priority, and executory contracts, and any special unsecured claims in the Plan. You will not list your unsecured debts. By including how much they are entitled to, as we will discuss below, that is considered treatment in the Plan.

Amount to Unsecured

Unsecured debts get whatever is left over after secured and priority claims have been paid in full (except for non-dischargeable debts), and that could range from getting nothing (at 0 percent) to getting more than what was owed (at 100 percent plus 7 percent interest). You will determine how much you will pay to your unsecured creditors by dividing the amount of unsecured creditors you have by the number of leftover funds you have to pay them.

If you did not have to complete the Means Test on the Chapter 13 B 22C form, you will just abide by the Plan unsecured amount. If you did complete the Chapter 13 Means Test, you may be required to pay your unsecured creditors what your disposable income is over 60 months. On the other hand, you may have to find how much you can pay by dividing your unsecured debts by the amount you have available. In most cases, this is determined by whichever amount yields a larger figure.

Attorney Fees

You will need to disclose how much you have paid your attorney to the point of filing, and how much is left to be paid to the attorney on your Plan. For instance, if you paid your attorney $200 out of a $3,000 fee, you would list $200 paid, $2,800 still owed, and list the total of $3,000.

The attorney is also required to file an income statement of their own attesting to these figures. The attorney will present this to you as a sort of "contract", meaning you understand the attorney's rate and how much has been paid thus far. You will sign this, and the form will be submitted with your packet upon filing.

Other Factors

Leases

In some districts, you need to address your executory contracts, or auto leases. Even though they are not a secured claim, or technically not your property, they still may need to be listed.

Non-dischargeable Debts

You may need to list how you plan to pay non-dischargeable debts upon completion of your plan.

Direct to Creditor Payments

Some districts allow debtors to make their own payments on certain obligations. Your leased vehicle, car purchase, or mortgage payment are some of the options for this; not every district allows it. Most that do allow it require you to be current on said obligation before Confirmation to be allowed to pay this obligation directly.

The advantage of paying these directly would be maintaining good faith with this creditor. While they are aware of the bankruptcy, the fact that you are current and desire to maintain these payments on your own may be to your benefit. On the other hand, making one payment to one source is much easier than remembering to pay the trustee, the mortgage company, and the car company.

Changes to Plan

This is where you have to be careful when filing your Plan. Most districts have a model, or typical, plan which they use for most Chapter 13 cases. These Plans may have different provisions based on local bankruptcy rules (or LBRs). If your particular case warrants one of these provisions to be changed or negated, you must list this as a change on the Plan.

Proof of Claims

This is where we welcome back those Chapter 7 filers who skipped the Chapter 13 Plan portion of this chapter.

Now is the time when the creditors fight back. Even though

you have listed all your creditors in your schedules, and now your plan, they are allowed to file a proof of claim. This will allow them to tell their side of the story, so to speak.

A proof of claim is a form the creditor fills out stating what they believe their debt is valued at. Frequently, the proof of claim will include backup of the documents you signed when you entered into the agreement, or contract, with the creditor.

The amount on the proof of claim may not always match with what you have listed in your Plan or schedules, and this is where issues may spring up with your case.

Possible Proof of Claim Issues

Proof of claims could significantly skew a bankruptcy case. If you severely underestimate the arrearages on your home mortgage, and then the proof of claim comes in much higher, this could cause your case to become infeasible, under-funded, and possibly be dismissed.

In a Chapter 13, a claim could come in as secured when you scheduled it as unsecured. If you were only offering 50 percent to your unsecured creditors, and an unsecured debt proof of claim comes in treating itself as secured, it could also cause problems for your case. This is because you have a debt that you scheduled to be paid half of what is owed now being paid in full. This situation will most likely result in a payment increase to keep the Plan moving.

In a Chapter 7, a creditor may file a proof of claim as well. They will only receive payment if you have had property liquidated. Even if you do not, creditors will occasionally file a proof of claim, but since you have no assets, they will receive nothing.

Objection to Proof of Claim

In some districts, the proof of claim is paramount, while in others, the Plan and schedules rule. This means that in certain areas, if a proof of claim comes in at more than what the debt was scheduled at, after the Plan and schedules have been filed, the trustee will use the proof of claim as treatment. If this seriously affects your plan, something may need to be done.

If a proof of claim comes in different than what has been scheduled, a good bankruptcy attorney knows how to deal with it.

What they do, or you if you represent yourself, is to file an objection to the proof of claim with the court. This means they disagree with the creditor's claim for a variety of reasons. It could be the treatment they are giving themselves (for example, unsecured debt proof of claim coming in as secured) or that their figuring of the debt does not correspond with what you or your attorney has figured as your debt for this creditor.

Many times, this objection will not get to court. If you have a legitimate concern, your attorney and the creditor will hash out an agreement to reduce the debt on the proof of claim. It will more than likely be more than what you had originally scheduled, but also less than what the creditor had claimed on their proof of claim.

Other times, the two parties will be unable to reach an

agreement and have to take the dispute before the bankruptcy judge, which was assigned to you and whom you appeared before for your Confirmation hearing. The judge will then decide who he sides with based on the merits of the issue brought before him or her by your attorney and the creditor's attorney.

Bar Date

We talked about how you need to file a matrix in Chapter 5. This is so all your creditors have notice of your case and can file a proof of claim if they are so inclined.

Your creditors have a short period of time for which they can file a proof of claim. They do not get to wait the entire period of the bankruptcy to get around to eventually filing a claim. Imagine going through four or four and a half years of a Chapter 13 bankruptcy case, which has worked, and a discharge is looming on the horizon, then suddenly a proof of claim comes in that totally skews your case and ultimately denies your discharge.

This is why there is a proof of claim bar date. For all creditors in a Chapter 7, and most in a Chapter 13, that bar date is 90 days from the date of filing of the case. Governmental units, such as the IRS or state taxing authority, are allowed 180 days to file a proof of claim in a Chapter 13.

After the bar date, your creditors may not file a proof of claim. If they do, it will simply be disallowed. As with everything in bankruptcy, there is an exception to this rule. If you did not include this creditor on your matrix, or the creditor can prove proof that proper notice of the bankruptcy was not sent out, a judge may allow the proof of claim.

So there you have it: the Chapter 13 Plan and proofs of claim. We now have thoroughly gone over the basic documents you will run into during your bankruptcy case. There may be others in a more complicated case, but you will more than likely run into all the documents we so painstakingly talked about over the last few chapters.

Now it is time to discuss the changes in the bankruptcy code that could affect your case.

CHAPTER 8

Recent Bankruptcy Changes

"Everything Changes but Change."
– Israel Zangwell, British Writer

We have discussed the changes in the bankruptcy code since 2005 briefly in this book. We will devote a little more to it in this chapter so you get an idea of some of the things that have changed since October 18, 2005, when the new code took hold.

If you know someone who filed for bankruptcy a number of years ago, they may not be helpful to you as you pursue your own case. This is because they may have filed before the new code took affect and, as such, were bound by slightly different rules and regulations.

To give you an understanding of the road to the new code, we should take a brief look at bankruptcy itself.

Bankruptcy History

Bankruptcy may be older than you realize.

Some people mistakenly think it was part of President

Franklin Delano Roosevelt's New Deal introduced in the 1930s to try to pry the country out of the doldrums of the Depression.

Bankruptcy, or forms of the practice, dates back to biblical times. The Old Testament talks of the Hebrew law of debt forgiveness:

"At the end of every seven years you are to cancel the debts of those who owe you money. This is how it is done. Everyone who has lent money to his neighbor is to cancel the debt: he must not try to collect the money: the Lord himself has declared the debt canceled."

It is extremely tough to file a proof of claim when the Lord says you cannot. This passage can be found in the book of Deuteronomy 15:1-2 and asks for people's debts to be forgiven every seven years.

It has never been fully determined where the word "bankruptcy" came from. Some say it has Latin roots with bancus (a bench or table) ruptus (broken). The earliest banks were simply a small stand, table, or bench which was set up in public areas, such as marketplaces. Simply put, if an earlier banker ran out of money, it was said that the banker "broke his bench," or, in modern day terms, went bankrupt. Other theories have the term originating in Italy, (banco rotto, meaning broken bank) France, or ancient Rome.

Even in the more conservative cultures, such as the Far East, bankruptcies were common in history. There is mention of bankruptcy in the ancient Mongolian Empire. If you think filing a motion to impose the stay on a third filed case in a year is a tough provision, imagine befalling the fate of a Mongolian filing three bankruptcies in a lifetime: death.

Anyone who has read Dickens knows England had debtors' prisons. If you could not pay your bills, you were thrown in jail. While there was a form of bankruptcy protection for the English, it was much geared toward the creditors. When starting their own country, early Americans knew this was not the way to treat their citizens.

Here in the United States, our forefathers had the foresight to include bankruptcy in the Constitution. Article 1, Section 8 lays out the duties of Congress. Clause 4 in this section states: "To establish [a] uniform Rule of Naturalization, and uniform Laws on the subject of Bankruptcies throughout the United States." The implementation of bankruptcy is laid out in statute law, which is included in the United States Code, where we get our bankruptcy laws.

Early American bankruptcy did not look much like it does today, or did even before 2005. In 1898, the first major bankruptcy reform bill took place, and for the first time, debtors were allowed to claim exemptions, and many previous non-dischargeable debts were now able to be discharged. The 1898 Bankruptcy Act was tweaked in 1938 by the Chandler Act, which set up the forerunners to the Chapter 11 and 13 processes, but most provisions in the act lasted 80 years.

The next major bankruptcy bill was the Bankruptcy Act of 1978. This bill solidified the different types of bankruptcies a corporation could qualify for into one – a Chapter 11. It also set up a federal system to oversee the local trustees and extended the authority of the bankruptcy courts and its judges. The Chapter 13 process was refined and made easier for individuals to file for instead of a Chapter 7.

With that act in mind, a rather remote practice was suddenly made mainstream. Filings soared in the 1980s and early 1990s until 1994, when reforms were made to the 1978 act, urging more people into filing a Chapter 13.

Bankruptcy Abuse Prevention and Consumer Protection Act of 2005

As of March 2008, a Gallop Poll showed that Congress had an approval rating of 21 percent. This is because Congress often does things that they feel is best for the country without consulting their constituents or industrial insiders for their input. This was the case with the Bankruptcy Abuse Prevention and Consumer Protection Act (or BAPCPA).

Congress took the advice of the high-priced lobbyists from the credit card and banking industries to implement laws that make no sense to many bankruptcy insiders. Congress failed to listen to many bankruptcy experts in formulating the law and instead, went forward with the legislation.

As you might expect with non-experts writing a law for an area they know nothing about, the law was poorly written and has added many frivolous and costly steps, such as the credit counseling pre-filing and before discharge.

Their intent was to make it harder for individuals to walk

away from their debts by forcing more people into filing a Chapter 13 and limiting Chapter 7 cases.

Nearly three years after the BAPCPA, 85 percent of those qualified for a Chapter 7 on October 16 (the day before the changeover) would still be eligible under the new code.

With statistics like this in mind, many bankruptcy insiders think the act has failed.

Finally, one of the biggest complaint lawyers have post-BAPCPA is the increased amount of "busy work," which consists of more menial forms and paperwork to be filed with cases. This busy work then drives up attorney fees.

We have touched on some of the changes already, but have not mentioned others. Here is a list of changes.

Mandatory Credit Counseling

As we discussed previously, you must obtain credit counseling before and during filing.

Additional Filing and Paperwork

Most districts in the country have gone to electronic case filing, where instead of going to the courthouse to file things, you, or more likely your attorney, will go to a computer and upload scores of documents that have been scanned. Sure, the court house is going paperless, but you and your attorney have more paperwork than ever before.

There are many rather pointless pieces of paperwork you must file when filing your case now that you did not have to pre-BAPCPA. We covered this paperwork in Chapter 5.

Fewer Automatic Protections for Debtors

Under the old code, several procedures would have been abandoned or delayed, but under the new code, they go forth.

Here are some of the examples of this:

- Delaying or stopping an eviction

- Automatically stopping a foreclosure on your home (held off for only 30 days for second case in a year, not held off at all in a third or additional case in a year)

- You must wait eight years from a discharge in a Chapter 7 before filing for another Chapter 7. This was increased by two years from the old code.

The Means Test

We discussed the Means Test thoroughly in Chapter 6.

Restricted Chapter 7 Eligibility

Going hand in hand with the Means Test is the decreased eligibility for a Chapter 7. Before BAPCPA, a debtor could file just about any bankruptcy they wanted (between a Chapter 7 and 13). Now higher income earners are forced into a Chapter 13.

As we saw with our example family, the Johnsons, the family just barely missed out on the eligibility for a Chapter 7 and was required to file for a Chapter 13.

Chapter 13 Disposable Income Subject to Means Test

Under the old code, Chapter 13 debtors' Plan payments were determined by their disposable income on Schedule J, but now they must subject that income to a Means Test if they fail to make less than the median income.

Property Valuation (Primarily for Chapter 7 cases)

Items and properties are valued at how much it would cost to replace the item instead of at the auction value. This means post-BAPCPA debtors have a greater risk of having their property liquidated by the trustee than their pre-BAPCPA counterparts.

Length of Time Living in One State in Order to Use Exemptions

Before BAPCPA, debtors' would use the exemptions of the state they are filing in for their exemptions. That is, provided they have lived in that state for "the better part" of 180 days, which simply means 91 or more days; this provision has not changed. If they have relocated recently, this could affect their ability to use their current state's exemptions, for better or worse.

The word "abuse" is prominent in the name of the bankruptcy reform act: Bankruptcy Abuse and Prevention and Consumer Protection Act. Congress alleged more widespread abuse of the bankruptcy system than people in the bankruptcy world saw, and this was one of their chief concerns: that people would be bucking the system to find a more liberal state exemption.

One cannot imagine someone struggling to pay their bills, yet having the money for an expensive move across the country with the sole idea of getting a more favorable bankruptcy filing. Apparently Congress could.

Here are the residency requirements:

- If you have lived in your current state for at least two years, you may use the state exemptions.

- If you have lived in your current state for 91 days up until two years, you will use the exemptions of the state in which you previously lived for the better part of 180 days prior to your current state.

- If the state you currently reside in offers the federal exemptions, you may use these, regardless of what state you came from originally.

- If your former state only offers its exemptions to in-state residents, and you are excluded, you can use the federal exemptions, regardless of whether they are available in your current state or not.

- If you have purchased a residence in your current state less than 40 months before your filing date, your homestead exemption may cap at $136,875, regardless of what is available in your current state.

We will discuss homestead exemptions in further detail in the next chapter.

Fewer and More Expensive Lawyers

This sounds like the start of a bad lawyer joke, but having fewer bankruptcy lawyers may actually be a good thing.

Like with any industry, there are some bad eggs out there, and faced with the increased workload, some of those bad eggs have chosen to move to other avenues. The downside with this is that competent attorneys have to charge their clients more because of the increased man hours involved.

Ineligible for a Discharge in Some Instances

Prior to BAPCPA, there were no limits on how many cases you could file in a short amount of time.

We have discussed the ramifications of filing multiple cases within a year, and how the automatic stay is not automatically implemented for the duration starting with the second case. Now we will address cases filed within a few years.

If you file for a Chapter 13 after obtaining a Chapter 7 discharge less than four years before, you are not eligible for a discharge in your Chapter 13 case. This means that you can take part in the Chapter 13 process and catch up on your bills with the benefit of the automatic stay; you will just not get the benefit of a discharge.

Bare in mind that all your debts will be essentially non-dischargeable, including any unsecured debts that have not received 100 percent in this bankruptcy case. Those creditors can still try to get the remainder of their money from you after your bankruptcy has concluded.

Honestly though, if you have been granted a discharge less than four years ago in a Chapter 7, you should not have any debts outside of perhaps your mortgage and your vehicle or vehicles. Sure emergencies happen, even to post-bankruptcy people, but if you have had unsecured debts accumulate since the discharge of the prior case, then something is wrong.

If you ran out after your Chapter 7 discharge and got credit card after credit card (yes, you will get pre-approved for some credit cards) and charged each to the max requiring you to file another bankruptcy, this time a Chapter 13 (because you are not entitled to a Chapter 7 for eight years), then you did not learn your lesson the first time around.

We will discuss the proper way to handle yourself post-discharge in Part III of this book.

CHAPTER 9

Foreclosure Process, Tax Liens, & Homestead Exemptions

"A house is made of walls and beams; a home is built with love and dreams."
– Unknown

No one wants to lose their home. The above quote is perfect to describe your house, which you lovingly refer to as your home.

Your home could be the first place you owned on your own, with no help from anyone else. Your home could be where you carried your new bride over the threshold when you were first married, or perhaps you were that blushing bride. Your home could be the place you laid your first born down to their first night's sleep in their warm, cozy, and colorful bedroom. Your home could be where you celebrated your team's championship by running into the neighborhood in joyful merriment. Your home could also be where you dealt with sadness, such as the loss of a loved one. Your home could cause you much frustration with constant repairs, both minor and major. Your home could be where you first saw your son or daughter in their baby pajamas, before their first day of school, in their cap and gown, and in their tuxedo or wedding dress. Your home could be the first place you held your first cooing grandchild.

Whether they are happy or sad, your house is at the backdrop for many of your memories. Whether you are single and only owned your house for a few years or you are married and lived in your home for 30 years and watched your family grow, this house is your home.

It is a tough truth to face. To lose your home after a lifetime of memories because of emergencies, mistakes, financial missteps, or predatory lending practices is almost unbearable. No matter your circumstances, you must face this truth, and if you are in such financial dire straight that you are behind on your mortgage payments, your home is in danger of being lost.

This is why it is important to understand and master the bankruptcy process. If you are open and honest during your bankruptcy, and you are truly willing to make it work, it will be tough for anyone to take your house.

To further help you learn about your home's role in a bankruptcy, we will talk in this chapter about a few key areas in the process which affect your home.

We will first discuss the foreclosure process.

Foreclosure

Sadly, the foreclosure rate is at an all-time high. Most industry insiders point to predatory lending practices and adjustable rate mortgage (ARM) loans as the main culprit, and they are not wrong, but they seem to ignore another larger issue: rising gas prices.

As of March 2008, the national average gas price was $3.26 per gallon. In March 2007, the number was at $2.51. That is quite a jump in one year. Also consider the average price per gallon in the year 2000: $1.31.

The dramatic price increases since 2000, and particularly since 2007, have forced many consumers to tighten their belts.

With higher gas costs come increased prices on things shipping by truck, train, or airplane, which requires gas; that includes everything. Grocery prices are just one thing that has skyrocketed because of the gas prices. One thing that does not increase because of gas prices are wages.

Some people are faced with skipping a payment on their mortgage to pay for their gas, which will allow them to go to and from work to be able to afford the mortgage or to put food on the table for their family; it is a vicious cycle. Mortgage companies are rarely understanding of their customers' issues and start foreclosure proceedings fairly rapidly, even after missing only one payment.

Process

Every state has its own timelines for foreclosures, but for the most part, the process is similar.

At some point after missing a payment or a few payments,

your mortgage company will contact you via certified letter telling you they have started foreclosure proceedings. They will more often than not give you a payoff figure on the letter or give you a phone number to call to obtain this figure. Sometimes you will call the lender, and other times, you will call the attorney firm handling the foreclosure.

If you do not bring the account current by the date listed on the letter, a sale, commonly called a "sheriff's sale," will take place at a municipal building in your county.

This is when many bankruptcies are filed, before the sheriff's sale, sometimes just hours before. If you contact an attorney telling them of your need to file for bankruptcy to prevent the sheriff's sale, the attorney will file an emergency petition on your behalf. This means they will most likely only file the bare necessities, such as the petition, and file the remainder of your documents soon after.

Do not wait for the sale to happen, though. It is extremely difficult to get a foreclosure sale reversed once a bankruptcy is filed; it is easier to have it stopped than reversed. Some debtors still file for bankruptcy after the sheriff's sale, but most acknowledge that their property has been sold and surrender it in their plan. By surrendering a property, it may allow you to file for a Chapter 7 instead of a Chapter 13.

If someone purchases the property, you go into what is called a "redemption period." The redemption period allows people to remain in their homes after the sale for a period of time. Not all states have a redemption period; you are given only a few days to pack your belongings and vacate the premises. Other states offer extensive redemptions periods.

This period of time, if you have come to terms with losing your home, can be quite helpful. You are able to save the money you would be sending in to the mortgage company, and you are able to seek out new living arrangements during this time.

On the other hand, if you are not giving up the fight, you can negotiate with your mortgage company to remain on the property. Mortgage companies have much more incentive to work with troubled mortgage holders these days because of the tremendous numbers of foreclosures nationwide. The mortgage company would rather have some money from you than be responsible for another one of thousands of unsold foreclosed homes in the country.

Options in Redemption Period

Obviously, since this is a book about bankruptcy, you can file for bankruptcy. As we pointed out, though, it becomes fairly tricky after a sheriff's sale has taken place. If you do not want to file bankruptcy, you have a few other options at this point.

Attempt a Short Sale

You could put your home on the market and attempt to sell it for a reasonable amount. "Reasonable amount" does not necessarily mean the current value of your home. If you work with a broker who has experience in short sales, the broker may be able to negotiate with the lender for a price they would be satisfied in receiving if the property is sold.

By going down this avenue, you are able to walk away

from your home on your own terms instead of from a foreclosure.

One problem with this method is that you have a short window of time to sell your home that corresponds with the redemption period. A buyer must be willing to close immediately, and that scares some buyers away. A buyer may have to sell their own property first, and likely will not have the means to pay for their new mortgage and the mortgage on the property they are selling. Once you get into the closing window of a month before the end of the redemption period, a short sale is extremely unlikely. Even immediate closings take a couple of weeks.

Another problem with this method is the terrible state of the United States housing market; it will be tough to find a buyer. This has largely to do with the foreclosure rates. There are so many properties for sale in the country that buyers can be choosey, and as our country enters a recession, the buyers become increasingly fewer.

Repayment Plan

You can attempt to obtain a payment plan from your lender, but chances are, you have tried this at some point in the foreclosure process and gotten nowhere.

A repayment plan is what it sounds like, a series of payments to help you catch up on your mortgage payment. If you can afford this with your ongoing payments, more power to you. Though, most consumers in this situation cannot afford this option.

Foreclosure Bailout

You may be able to find a lender who will loan you the money to catch up on your mortgage; this is exceedingly tricky though. Way back in the first chapter, we talked of that notion of "taking from Peter to pay Paul." This is exactly what this option is.

Yes, you will save your home, but now you have two large payments each month. Ask yourself whether you will be able to afford both of these payments in the long run. You could be back in this same position three or six months or a year from now.

Expiration of Redemption Period

After the redemption period ends, the eviction process begins. For some states, this will be immediate, but for others, you may have a brief period of time before the county police or other officials arrive on your property to remove you.

In some instances, you will be allowed to attend a court date and request a trial to save your home, but at this point in the process, these are rarely successful.

We have gone to immense lengths in this book to encourage you to not be embarrassed by filing for bankruptcy. On the other hand, if you stay in your home with all your belongings, and the authorities put you out of your home, there is nothing more embarrassing.

The authorities have the right to forcefully remove you and your belongings. Your belongings are simply carried out and thrown on the curb for all neighbors and passersby to see. Also, your belongings are now fair game for anyone to take, so if you happen not to be at your home when the authorities arrive, expect people to take many of your belongings.

For these reasons, it is important that you accept the situation you are involved in and take action before it comes to this. There is nothing more embarrassing than you and your belongings being literally kicked to the curb, and no advice from a book can soften this blow for you.

Tax Liens

We know that the basis of many of your debts you have are from liens, but luckily, most of these liens are addressed in bankruptcy so that the lien holder cannot take your home.

Tax liens, sometimes called levies, are different. Bankruptcies prevent the IRS from coming after you for a tax lien, but they, unlike any other lien holders, have the benefit of having their debts less than three years old being non-dischargeable. So even after your bankruptcy case concludes, if you have back taxes, they can seize your house.

While that is rare, it could happen. The IRS first withholds your tax refunds. If that is not enough to pay your debt, they will garnish your wages and even your bank account before attempting to claim the house. They may even go after your cars and any luxury items, such as RVs or motorcycles, before taking your house.

One can imagine the IRS, much like the mortgage companies, do not want to have a vacant property they must sell in a down real estate market, but do not count on this factor to save your home from the IRS.

The process for the IRS is the same as it would be for a mortgage company. They would seek foreclosure by holding a public auction, or sheriff's sale.

If you are able to sell your home in a short sale, the IRS will be first in line to take what is owed.

Homestead Exemptions

After all the negativity of this chapter, it is nice to talk about a positive aspect: homestead exemptions in bankruptcy.

Homestead exemptions range significantly in value and are based on state levels. Some states, Texas and Florida for instance, have an unlimited exemption.

No Equity

If you have no equity in your home, you will not risk losing your home, as long as you continue to make the payments if a lien has been implemented. So if you filed for a Chapter 7 bankruptcy, the trustee will not sell your house because there will be no profit made.

Some Equity

If you have a little equity in your home, chances are you will be completely protected by your state's homestead exemption. Once again, if there is no available equity for a Chapter 7 trustee to go after, they will not bother to sell your home. Even if it is slightly over the exemption, the trustee will have to factor in their costs of selling the property and come to the conclusion that it is not worth a sale.

A Large Amount of Equity

This could be troublesome if you file for a Chapter 7. With the exceptions of the states that offer complete homestead exemptions, you risk having your home being sold by the Chapter 7 trustee, which is why many in this situation opt for filing a Chapter 13.

In these types of Chapter 13 cases, be warned that the amount you have to pay for your unsecured debts is tied directly into what you would have paid those creditors in a Chapter 7.

For instance, if your equity is so enormous that after your homestead exemption is taken into account, you have $20,000 available to be disbursed to your creditors in a Chapter 7, the Chapter 13 trustee will ask for at least the $20,000 and possibly interest to be paid to your unsecured creditors.

Reducing your Equity

You can take steps to reduce the equity in your home, but bear in mind that if you desire to file bankruptcy right now, these steps are not for you. In some instances, like refinancing your home, you will have to wait at least 90 days before filing for bankruptcy.

You could:

- Refinance for more than you currently owe

- Obtain a home equity loan

- Resort to legalized bribery: that is, pay to the Chapter 7 trustee the amount they would receive from the sale of your home by selling some of your other exempt property (selling your non-exempt property just prior to a bankruptcy is a no-no) or from income received after filing

The best option is to not reduce your equity. Just file for a Chapter 13 and save yourself any of the above grief.

CHAPTER 10

Bankruptcy Fraud, Myths, and Frequently Asked Questions

"The art and science of asking questions is the source of all knowledge."
– Adolf Berle 1937-1971, American Politician

It is especially important to ask many questions when referring to the bankruptcy process.

Bankruptcy is a complex, anxious, and worrisome (insert any feelings you are having that have not been included) process. For someone with little to no knowledge of bankruptcy law and circumstances, it can be downright frightening.

We have discussed much of the ins and outs of bankruptcy, but most of this chapter will be about what should not happen in bankruptcy by way of fraudulent filings and myths about certain things required or not required of you in bankruptcy. Finally, we will list some common questions you may have regarding your filing and answer them to attempt to calm your fears.

Bankruptcy Fraud

When you sign the paperwork before, and occasionally during, your bankruptcy, you sign this under the "penalty of perjury." This is the same perjury you would be charged with when appearing in a courtroom as a witness in a legal proceeding. If you knowingly lied on the stand, and it was later proven that you lied, you would be held liable for the penalty of perjury. Signing this paperwork is no different.

Common Types

Do not take the approach of "if the trustee does not ask about a particular item or piece of property, than they do not need to know about it." You need to be as forthcoming in a bankruptcy case as you would in a lawsuit or a criminal proceeding.

Many people make the mistake of not realizing that bankruptcy is a court case, backed by the United States Justice Department, just like those other proceedings. By making this mistake, people think they can be less than forthcoming in their bankruptcy and nothing will happen to them. Do not think this way.

Here are some examples of common bankruptcy fraud:

- Failure to disclose all your property

- Failing to disclose all your income

- Selling non-exempt property before filing

- Misrepresenting yourself by given a false name, alias, or social security number

- Writing personal checks to the trustee and then stopping payment on the checks

- Claiming a piece of property as your own when it actually belonged to someone else or was rented

There are some other circumstances that technically could be considered fraudulent behavior on the debtors' behalf, but more likely will simply result in a dismissal.

Possibly in these cases, the trustee or your creditors will seek a 180-day bar from filing for future bankruptcy cases, so you cannot simply re-file after committing fraud, or in less harsh terms for the lesser types of actions listed below, bad faith.

Here are types of situations considered bad faith:

- Selling or refinancing your home without seeking approval (because trustee will want to use the proceeds to pay off your unsecured creditors)

- Obtaining credit over $1,000 without seeking approval

- Changing a job without informing the trustee (because your income may have increased and will allow you to pay more into the plan)

- Moving and not informing the trustee of your new address

- Getting a monetary judgment from a lawsuit and not informing the trustee

Penalties

Do not think that if you get caught lying in a bankruptcy, you will only get a slap on the wrist.

Criminal prosecutions for fraud in bankruptcy were rare under the old code, but the new code has provisions that make prosecution much easier. In addition, under the new code, one out of 250 cases is selected for an audit, which means you may be required to submit even more paperwork.

Here are some examples of individuals getting prosecuted for being less than forthcoming with their bankruptcy information:

- A Massachusetts debtor was recently given jail time for failing to list the condominium he owned and omitted jewelry totaling $26,000.

- Again, a Massachusetts debtor was thrown in jail because she undervalued her home value, which was $116,000, at $70,000.

- A debtor from Alaska had to serve time for not including cash and diamonds that had been buried.

- A Pennsylvania woman went to jail because she did not list her $50,000 divorce settlement.

No one wants to serve jail time on top of their financial woes.

If the above examples do not convince you to file honestly, you should most likely refrain from filing. Bankruptcy has several levels, and each level has thousands of pairs of eyes looking at your documents. The odds of successfully filing and discharging a fraudulent Chapter 7 case are not good. Even more remote is the possibility of not getting caught with fraud in a Chapter 13 case, which has more hearings than a Chapter 7 and could last five years.

If you are honest and sincere about your case, you will gain many allies in your bankruptcy. File in bad faith or commit fraud, and watch the enemies line up to make your life worse than you could have ever imagined.

Bankruptcy Myths

There are some misconceptions about bankruptcy that people who have never experienced it may have.

You have made it through over nine chapters of this book and are now extremely well-versed in bankruptcy, so some of these items will be review for you.

Nevertheless, this section may be a good thing to show your friends and relatives who do not quite understand the bankruptcy process, and may have these myths in mind when they are trying to advise you whether to file for bankruptcy.

MYTH #1: Individuals can no longer file for bankruptcy after the new code was passed

By you reading this book, you know this not to be true,

but you would be surprised how many believe this today, several years after the implementation of BAPCPA in October 2005. This was especially the case immediately following the first months of post-BAPCPA.

If you could recall the news coverage the changeover received in the fall of 2005, you would remember long lines of people standing outside the bankruptcy court buildings to file on the eve before the changeover to the new code. This coverage, along with the common misconception that the new laws made it so tough that almost no one could file for bankruptcy anymore, led to this belief.

Many attorneys had to step up their advertisements to educate people wallowing in debt that they still could file for bankruptcy.

So yes, you can file for bankruptcy.

MYTH #2: Bankruptcy will erase all my credit and I will have a spotless credit record

While you hear much about getting a "fresh start," it is not the freshest of starts. The debts you had on your credit report will have a note in each creditor that the debt was paid by your bankruptcy and that it was discharged this way.

Your bankruptcy itself will claim residency on your credit report for up to ten years.

Your fresh start will be from the aspect that you can breathe easier with no one hounding you for payment anymore, but there are ramifications, such as difficulty obtaining credit or obtaining credit at a reasonable interest rate.

MYTH #3: Your credit will be ruined for the rest of your life

Piggybacking on the last myth, yes, your credit will take a hit – for a while. Having a bankruptcy on your credit report is no more damaging than having many unpaid credit accounts appearing on the report. Eventually, things will normalize and you will be able to achieve credit once again. You just need to be patient.

MYTH #4: You should be ashamed of yourself

Actually, the person telling you this myth should be the one ashamed of themselves. You are being proactive and not letting your debt situation sink you. If you are filing a Chapter 13, you want to pay back some or all of your debts. If you are filing a Chapter 7, you just need a second chance at things. America was built on second chances. Keep your chin up.

MYTH #5: You are only entitled to one bankruptcy in your lifetime

Not true. With the exception of having to wait eight years between Chapter 7 cases, you can file for bankruptcy as many times as you need during your life.

Chapter 13 cases are essentially endless, though as we discussed, you may not be guaranteed the precious automatic stay if multiple cases have occurred within one year. We also learned that if you have received a Chapter 7 discharge less than four years before filing a Chapter 13, you will not receive a discharge in the current Chapter 13, but you are still eligible to file, and in that case, able to have the automatic stay.

Please note, a judge may see numerous cases as a debtor's way of bucking the system, so please be mindful of this when filing multiple cases.

MYTH #6: Everything you have will be taken

You may lose some items in a Chapter 7, and you may be forced to part with some luxury items, such as time shares, RVs, ATVs, or jet skis in a Chapter 13, but you will not lose your essentials, provided you have enough exemptions available.

MYTH #7: A Chapter 7 is better than a Chapter 13

This is a myth, but not because we are saying a Chapter 13 is better than a Chapter 7. Chapter 7, with its rather brief period and no payments, has an advantage if you skim the surface of the types of bankruptcies. You are also able to see that Chapter 13 has distinct advantages as well, one being no possibility of having your property sold. This is a personal decision for you and your family. We discussed making this important decision back in Chapter 2, and it is your decision to make.

Frequently Asked Questions

Ask many questions of the people involved with your bankruptcy. Ask your attorney and trustee many questions, particularly, at the 341 Meeting. There is no such thing as a stupid question.

Here are some frequently asked questions you may have:

I am involved in a Chapter 13 case and I filed jointly with my husband, but now we are thinking about getting divorced. How will this affect our case? Do we need permission to get a divorce?

Answering the last question first: no, a bankruptcy judge does not have the power to order a couple desiring a divorce to stay together.

Preferably, if you are on the road to divorce prior to filing a bankruptcy, you may want to wait for the divorce proceeding to at least be started before filing for bankruptcy. Preferably, you should wait until the conclusion, because then the division of the married debts will have been completed. Sometimes, divorces can drag on for a long time, so waiting for the conclusion to file for bankruptcy is not always an option.

If you need to divorce in the middle of your Chapter 13 term, it could cause some difficulties. A Chapter 13 only allows a joint case for people who are married, and if you become divorced, your trustee can file a motion to dismiss. If you have an understanding trustee, he or she may ignore your divorce and allow your case to continue if you both are committed to maintaining the Plan and the payments.

As to how this affects your divorce, you will have to ask your divorce attorney. Most likely, you can ask the divorce court to hold off on dividing up the assets until the bankruptcy has been discharged.

So am I subject to local, state, or federal bankruptcy rules?

You are subject to all three sets of rules. Each local area has its own local rules that may slightly differ from district to district, but would they never supersede a state or federal bankruptcy rule. Local rules are normally outlined in some form in the particular district's Model Plan, or most frequently used Plan. You may obtain copies of state and local bankruptcy codes on the Internet, at your bankruptcy courthouse, or perhaps at your local library.

To What Degree Do I Have to Inform my Employer?

It depends on your district.

In some areas, you will be able to pay your debts directly or by having an automatic deduction out of your checking account once per month. This way, your employer does not have to know.

More commonly, a bankruptcy court will require a wage deduction be entered. This is sort of like a garnishment, but it is a voluntary garnishment. Your employer will send your Plan payment directly to the trustee out of your paycheck.

In these areas, though, you may file a motion to be excluded from this provision. If you genuinely feel your employer will fire you over a bankruptcy, then the trustee will not argue too much against this, as long as you agree to make your payments on your own and stay current.

If a creditor is already garnishing your wages, then your

employer already knows you have some financial troubles, so a bankruptcy deduction is not going to make much difference. Actually, your employer may think more highly of you because you are being proactive.

Bear in mind that if your employer fails to make the payments at any point, it is up to you to continue to make them or make them up, but if your employer continues to refuse to make the payments, you can get an order to show cause against them. They will have to appear before your judge and explain why they refuse to make this payment. Judges do not look too highly on employers pulling these shenanigans.

Okay, I know I should not be embarrassed, but I want my bankruptcy to be as little known as possible. I do not want my Great Aunt Delores bringing up my bankruptcy at Thanksgiving Dinner.

Rest assured, unless Great Aunt Delores reads law publications, or works for the bankruptcy court or the local trustee, she will not know about your bankruptcy.

One of the provisions of the new code was an attempt to shame people out of filing for bankruptcy by publishing the listings in a local newspaper. Do not expect to set this book down and go grab your highly circulated local paper with these listings above the fold on the front page. They simply are not there.

Bankruptcy listings are included in extremely low-circulated newspapers or magazines which are often trade publications, such as law magazines.

How Soon Should I Expect My Creditors to Stop Pestering Me After I File?

Your creditors should leave you alone within a few days. They will have to be allowed time to receive notice of your bankruptcy. With electronic filing common these days, it should not take long.

Give it a week for the calls to stop and a few weeks for the mail to stop (they may have mailed these correspondences before receiving notice). If they do not stop in this timeframe, contact your attorney immediately.

The ramifications of continuing to harass a debtor in bankruptcy could include punitive damages awarded to you.

Remember that if you are going it alone in your case, your creditors will still need to contact you to inquire about their status in the bankruptcy and attempt to negotiate. This would be one of the duties of your attorney, but as a Pro Se debtor, you must continue to deal with your creditors.

Most of my debts are my own, and I do not want to force my spouse to file with me. How will she be affected if she does not file with me?

Make sure you truly investigate to make sure that any of the debts that you are leaving out because you think they are your non-filing spouse's debt are truly your spouse's debt. If there are any joint debts in arrears, your spouse may have to bite the bullet and jointly file with you.

If your non-filing spouse simply co-signed on a loan that

is in bankruptcy, he or she could be affected. If this is an unsecured debt, and your bankruptcy allows for less than 100 percent, the creditor could still pursue collections against your spouse even while you are in bankruptcy.

It is because of this case that debtors in this situation give special status to these types of debts as "special unsecured," which is guaranteed to pay 100 percent and keep your spouse (or other co-signer) out of danger.

What happens if I miss some Plan payments?

Do not miss any payments. Emergencies happen, but the key is to be proactive in this situation. You will have to address this situation immediately.

If it was a mistake, and your employer forgot to take the deduction out of your paycheck, then you should have noticed this because your paycheck was more. Ideally, you saved this extra income and are in the process of sending it to the trustee. As long as you address this as soon as possible, the trustee understands in most instances.

On the other hand, if you begin to miss a series of payments, or begin to send in payments for less than you are required to be sending, the trustee may sense your inability to make the proposed Plan payments and begin dismissal proceedings.

If this is the case, you or your attorney may try to propose a few suggestions:

- Ask for the missed payments to be excused. The excuse for this had better be good, and most times, it comes with a catch – increased Plan payments going forward.

- Extend the Plan, as you may add some terms onto a 36-, 42-, or 48-month Plan to make up for the missing payments. Though, this is not an option in a 60-month Plan.

- Lump-sum payment. If you can come up with the entire amount of the missed payment, it will be "no harm, no foul," and your case will continue as was proposed.

I have heard there is a way to pay less on my vehicle in a Chapter 13 case, is this true?

Yes, some debts are allowed to be "crammed," which means you pay a secured portion of your vehicle based on its value and the rest of your debt is paid as unsecured.

For instance, if your vehicle has a blue book value of $8,000, but you owe $12,000, you can propose a cram down so that you pay 100 percent of the $8,000 and the remainder, the $4,000, is paid at whatever rate you are proposing to unsecured creditors.

There are some provisions for this:

- You must pay the secured portion off during the plan, meaning if you proposed a 36-month plan, and the debt is set to cure after the end of the plan, you must propose a plan that allows this debt to cure during the plan. So you will almost certainly have to propose a 60-month plan.

- You must keep the collateral in good shape.

- In most cases, the debtor has to agree to this treatment.

- The vehicle must be over 910 days old (or just under two and a half years).

I am looking into filing for Chapter 7, knowing full well some of my property may be liquidated by the trustee. I live alone with my cat, "Toonces," and he means the world to me. Since "Toonces" is technically my property, can the trustee sell him? I cannot live without "Toonces;" what will I do?

If you do not have a cat named "Toonces" or a dog named "Monty" or any other animal with a silly name, do not laugh at this question. Animals mean a good deal to people, and this is a common concern.

No, the trustee will not sell, or liquidate (that just sounds terrible), your precious pet. Yes, the animal is part of your property, but an old dog or a cat has no monetary value to anyone, it only has sentimental value to its owner.

Now if you have racing dogs or something like that, that could be a different story, but be comforted with the fact that "Toonces" is not going anywhere.

I cannot make ends meet anymore; I am going into the last year or so of my Chapter 13, can I be discharged early?

Not unless it is under extreme circumstances, but there is

a thing called a "hardship discharge." This is reserved for the death of a spouse, leaving you as an only parent, or an illness of a spouse, resulting in you having to leave your employment. Some people in military situations can receive a hardship discharge as well. There are more remote types of cases, but if you are seeking a hardship discharge, you will have to prove your hardship.

Your attorney is paramount in getting a hardship discharge if it is warranted. Lean on them to read the law, to find out whether you are eligible, and to argue before the judge the importance of receiving your hardship discharge.

Chances are, your question has not been answered here. It is impossible for people to know what is on your mind. Therefore, be sure to ask all the questions you have at any time in your bankruptcy process.

It is simple; failing to ask one pertinent question could be the difference between a successful bankruptcy case and a dismissal.

CHAPTER 11

What to Expect After Discharge

"Every accomplishment starts with the decision to try."
– Unknown

Congratulations are in order. You should be congratulated for making it this far. Many people may try bankruptcy, but many of them do not have the strength, the fortitude, the conviction, the courage, or the sense of urgency that you had throughout the process. You knew the importance of maintaining contact with your attorney and the trustee, making your payments in full and on time, and adhering to all the rules and regulations of the bankruptcy process.

Particularly if you filed for a Chapter 13 and are getting discharged, think back to your early court hearings. Most of the other debtors who were in the same boat as you at your 341 Meeting and your Confirmation hearing have long since been removed from bankruptcy, by their choice via a voluntary dismissal or by others through motions to dismiss.

You can take solace in the fact that you have made it through the arduous process of a bankruptcy. You probably never imagined this day would arrive when you decided to file, but if you are about to or have received your discharge, this monumental day is here.

If you had filed for a Chapter 7, it has only been a few months, but you felt the sting of being deeply in debt for a long time before filing. If you are a Chapter 13 debtor, you can now feel the release of that monkey off your back after many years of drowning in debt and living through the three to five years of being in bankruptcy.

As your discharge dawns and you begin to move through a life with little to no debt (you may still have some debts that survived the discharge), you will see the distinct advantages of post-bankruptcy life. While thinking this way, it is easy to overlook the fact that the protections and comfort the bankruptcy provided are now gone.

There is no doubt that filing for bankruptcy capped an incredibly hard time in your life, and it would be easy to see your bankruptcy as a negative experience. In time, you will likely look back on your bankruptcy as a positive turning point in your life. You could see it as the point when you took control over your financial life once and for all.

As you prepare for post-bankruptcy life and gear up to be a better, smarter consumer (which we will cover in the last Part of this book), there is some important information you will need to know, realize, and remember about life after bankruptcy.

Wave Adios to Your Old Friend: The Automatic Stay

The Automatic Stay, like the Lone Ranger, swoops in, saves the day, asks for no thanks, and quietly rides out of town.

The Automatic Stay was one of the first advantages we listed in favor of filing for bankruptcy way back in Chapter 2. You worked hard to prevent your bankruptcy from being dismissed before your discharge, because you knew of the circumstances involved in obtaining an automatic stay in recent multiple cases. It served its purpose by preventing creditors from bothering you or trying to collect debts from you, but now it is gone.

This means that if you begin to fall behind in your mortgage or car note, there is no protection from the hounding of those creditors. Also, if you have debts that have survived the discharge, such as child support payments, student loans, taxes, or any other non-dischargeable debt, expect the letters and calls to begin again fairly quickly.

Prepare yourself for this before it happens.

Attempting to Collect a Discharged Debt

Please be aware that any creditors discharged in the bankruptcy can not contact you regarding this debt. If an unsecured creditor is not happy about not getting anything in a Chapter 7, or much less than what was owed in a Chapter 13, they can not take that anger or frustration out by contacting, harassing, or suing you for payment.

Most of the large credit card companies, such as MBNA or Capital One, have experienced their customers filing bankruptcy many times before, so they take it in stride. On the other hand, private individuals who you owed money to who have had their debts wiped out, or were paid only a fraction of their debts, may not be as understanding. They may begin harassing you for the remainder of the debt. If they continue to harass you, politely inform them that it is against the law for them to contact you about this debt.

If you feel you did not accurately provide notice of the bankruptcy to this creditor, it may be another story, but if you are convinced that this creditor received proper notice of the bankruptcy and was well aware of the proceeding, they have no legal standing to harass you.

If you find yourself in these circumstances, you may wish to send the offending creditor some form of the following letter:

LETTER TO CREDITOR

777 Your Street
Florida City, FL 12345
May 20, 20xx
Bank of the Powerful and Wealthy
1234 Easy Street, Suite 900
Golden Shores, FL 12345

To Whom It May Concern,

Please allow this to serve as the first and only warning to your company to stop any and all correspondence to me about any debts you feel are owed to your company.

One of your associates, Todd Wilson, has contacted me a number of times at my home and work. He has also sent a letter to my residence. Mr. Wilson does not seem to know that the debt he has been contacting me on has been discharged in my bankruptcy. He is stating that the debt of $6394 is still due and delinquent on my old account with you, which had the account number of 7863-248-313-734.

The paperwork I have from my bankruptcy clearly shows your company had been properly noticed of this bankruptcy case 08-74391, which was filed in

> ### LETTER TO CREDITOR
>
> the Central District of Florida) on April 19, 20xx and discharged on June 9, 20xx. Please note your company has violated federal law, 11 U.S.C. § 524.
>
> I am fully protected under this law and will not hesitate to pursue my legal rights, which may, and rightfully could, include filing a lawsuit against your company for harassment.
>
> Sincerely,
>
> *Stacey Smith*
>
> Stacey Smith

Obviously, you will want to use your specific information pertaining to your name, case number, location, and offending creditor, but use this letter as a helpful template when responding to a harassing creditor.

If this does not get results, you may want to hire an attorney or visit your old bankruptcy attorney. Chances are, once they see an attorney is involved, the creditor will back off. If they do not, you are well within your rights to file a lawsuit in either district or bankruptcy court against the offending creditor.

In rare cases, an aggressive creditor like this will sue you. If this happens, you will want to counter sue the creditor. You have the upper hand here; you have a discharge order issued by the bankruptcy court as your defense.

Omitted Property or Property Acquired During Chapter 7

We discussed bad faith and fraudulent behavior in a bankruptcy proceeding in the last chapter. Just because the Chapter 7 is a short process in relation to a Chapter 13 does not mean you can get away with withholding information from the trustee.

If you discover that by error (or if you have come to your senses and decided it is time to be truthful), you omitted a piece of property or acquired a piece of property shortly after filing, you must inform the trustee immediately. If you do not, and the trustee does not find out until after discharge, they have the right to reopen your bankruptcy case.

Reopening of a Bankruptcy Case

This could happen in either bankruptcy, although it is exceedingly rare. The reason given above is one of the only reasons a Chapter 7 trustee would reopen a case. If they do not feel there will be enough revenue produced after offsetting the costs of reopening a case and the selling of the discovered property, they may not even bother.

A reopening of a Chapter 13 case may occur if a creditor can prove they never received notice of the bankruptcy. This is hard to prove, however, especially in a bankruptcy lasting for three to five years. It is almost impossible not to realize someone who owes you money is in a bankruptcy.

Revoking a Discharge

One step beyond reopening a case is revoking a discharge. This is generally only done when it is alleged that the discharge was brought about by fraudulent behavior during your bankruptcy. There are other even more rare circumstances, but if this happens, even if you went Pro

Se in your bankruptcy case, you need to hire an attorney to fight against this. Imagine the disaster of being out of bankruptcy for up to a year (the maximum amount of time the trustee could ask for this) and then having all your debts reinstated.

Play by the rules, and this will not happen. If it does, hire an attorney.

Discrimination

Perhaps you feel that your life will never be the same post-bankruptcy, that you will never be treated fairly once people see your credit report.

Perhaps this will reassure you. There is a law built within the bankruptcy code to protect debtors from this type of discrimination. The law number is 11 USC § 525: Protection against discriminatory treatment.

It is important to fully know your rights, so here is the law directly as it reads out of the Bankruptcy Code and Rules, 2008 Edition:

(a) Except as provided in the Perishable Agricultural Commodities Act, 1930, the Packers and Stockyards Act, 1921, and section 1 of the Act entitled "An Act making appropriations for the Department of Agriculture for the fiscal year ending June 30, 1944, and for other purposes," approved July 12, 1943, a governmental unit may not deny, revoke, suspend, or refuse to renew a license, permit, charter, franchise, or other similar grant to, condition such a grant to, discriminate with respect to such a grant against, deny employment to, terminate the employment of, or

discriminate with respect to employment against, a person that is or has been a debtor under this title or a bankrupt or a debtor under the Bankruptcy Act, or another person with whom such bankrupt or debtor has been associated, solely because such bankrupt or debtor is or has been a debtor under this title or a bankrupt or debtor under the Bankruptcy Act, has been insolvent before the commencement of the case under this title, or during the case but before the debtor is granted or denied a discharge, or has not paid a debt that is dischargeable in the case under this title or that was discharged under the Bankruptcy Act.

(b) No private employer may terminate the employment of, or discriminate with respect to employment against, an individual who is or has been a debtor under this title, a debtor or bankrupt under the Bankruptcy Act, or an individual associated with such debtor or bankrupt, solely because such debtor or bankrupt--

> *(1) is or has been a debtor under this title or a debtor or bankrupt under the Bankruptcy Act;*

> *(2) has been insolvent before the commencement of a case under this title or during the case but before the grant or denial of a discharge; or*

> *(3) has not paid a debt that is dischargeable in a case under this title or that was discharged under the Bankruptcy Act.*

(c)

> *(1) A governmental unit that operates a student grant or loan program and a person engaged in a business*

that includes the making of loans guaranteed or insured under a student loan program may not deny a grant, loan, loan guarantee, or loan insurance to a person that is or has been a debtor under this title or a bankrupt or debtor under the Bankruptcy Act, or another person with whom the debtor or bankrupt has been associated, because the debtor or bankrupt is or has been a debtor under this title or a bankrupt or debtor under the Bankruptcy Act, has been insolvent before the commencement of a case under this title or during the pendency of the case but before the debtor is granted or denied a discharge, or has not paid a debt that is dischargeable in the case under this title or that was discharged under the Bankruptcy Act.

(2) In this section, "student loan program" means any program operated under title IV of the Higher Education Act of 1965 or a similar program operated under State or local law.

Translated into non-attorney speak, what that means is no governmental unit has the ability to deny you any service or right because you filed for bankruptcy.

Government Discrimination

Remember this does not pertain to credit, but it does provide a good blanket of protection, which does not allow a government body to do the following events stemming from the filing of bankruptcy:

- Deny you employment or fire you

- Deny you or revoke your public benefits

- Evict you from public housing

- Deny the issuing of, or refuse to renew, a liquor license

- Fail to issue a college transcript

- Deny you a driver's license

- Deny you a government contract (such as a contract for your business)

- Deny you student loans

Non-government Discrimination

It is a little trickier in the private sector. If you will notice, the law above speaks to private employers as it does with government agencies. They may not fire you merely based on the fact that you have filed for bankruptcy, but you may notice that hiring is missing from the law. No law prevents an employer from not hiring you because of your bankruptcy. Some bankruptcy scholars argue that by there simply being a law that does not allow an individual to be fired, the same law applies to the hiring process.

Some employers ask applicants if they can do a background check, which may or may not include looking up their credit scores. If this is the case, you will have to sign an authorization form. You are not bound by this, but if you do not authorize this, you may not get the job. The best way to handle a situation like this is to tell the interviewer that you hit a rough patch in your life and had to seek bankruptcy protection. Nine times out of ten, this will catch the interviewer off guard and make them realize how honest you are. This may give you a leg up on the other candidates. Especially if they see that your bankruptcy was a few years back and you have had good credit since then.

Other instances of what you think is covered by this discrimination statue that may not be include renting an apartment. If your potential landlord does a credit check and denies your application, he or she is doing this on the basis of your credit, not because you filed for bankruptcy. If you had left your debts alone and done nothing, the same landlord would deny the application.

For this reason, if you can possibly come up with a few months worth of rent up front, a landlord may reconsider his decision. Do not let the landlord be surprised. Tell him what to expect when running the credit check and hash out any other options, such as paying a few months in advanced. Again, like the employer, the landlord may respect your honesty and it may sway them into accepting your application.

Be Ready for Credit Card Companies to Test You

You have wiped your credit clean. No more pesky credit card payments (or credit cards at all, because ideally, you cut them up after the filing of your case). You will notice something infiltrating your mailbox soon after a discharge in either chapter: credit cards.

Credit applications, pre-approved credit applications, and

even actual credit cards through the mail that can be activated with a simple call to an 800 number will begin arriving.

You may ask why in the world a credit card company would put out the invitation for you to obtain credit through them when you just got out of a bankruptcy, which either wiped your unsecured debts out with nothing paid in a Chapter 7, or a small fraction was paid in a Chapter 13. The answer is simple: you are an easy target.

These circumstances are more common post-Chapter 7, but also happen after a Chapter 13. You know that after you file for a Chapter 7, you have to wait eight years to file. Therefore, you have virtually no credit, and you do not have any recourse to dodge payment (except filing for a Chapter 13, in which there is a possibility of some payment).

Simply put, this is predatory lending. These credit card companies are preying on your perceived weakness: spending. Do not make this mistake. Cut these cards up and throw away the applications.

You have gone through a bankruptcy in order to obtain a fresh start. Do not let that fresh start grow stale before you are even out of the starting blocks of your new life. You have worked too hard to fall for these tactics.

This topic serves as a good closing point to Part II of this book and is a good preliminary point for the beginning of Part III.

This Part of the book dealt with the nuts and bolts of filing for bankruptcy, and we will now move to the final Part of the book, which will tell you how to gradually build your credit back to good standing and what to expect when obtaining a car loan or mortgage soon after your discharge.

PART III

POST FILING:
REBUILDING AND
RESTRUCTURING YOUR
LIFE AND CREDIT

CHAPTER 12

Recall How You Got Here and Begin Restructuring Your Spending Habits

"The only person who is educated is the one who has learned how to learn and change."
– *Carl Rogers, American Psychotherapist*

Stop what you are doing, take a breath, and realize how far you have come. When we began the journey of this book, you were deciding what to do, figuring out the circumstances that landed you here, and then filed for bankruptcy. We meandered our way through filling out documents and discussed court hearings, costs, and the importance of hiring an attorney. We discussed the new code, bankruptcy myths, and frequently asked questions, and implored you to ask as many questions as possible. Finally, we told you what you should expect as you approach, and ultimately receive, your long awaited discharge.

You have sacrificed much to get to this point, but you have a little way to go.

If you break the plane of the goal in football before fumbling, you still have a touchdown, but in the real world, people are not so lucky. If you fumble the ball in the "end zone" of post-bankruptcy, the sacrifices made leading up to and during bankruptcy will mean nothing. You have to set in a system that will work for you, and you will eventually achieve your ultimate goal of having a completely fresh start.

Remembering How You Got Here

We talked about this way back in Chapter 1. We saw how you got to the point where you were considering filing for bankruptcy. We discussed all the factors that might have been your fault and the ones that were out of your control.

For the people who had the unplanned events, such as hospital bills, a divorce, or other problems that came about not by poor spending, but by sheer happenstance, it may be easy for you to skip this last portion of the book because you do not think this applies to you. Do not make this mistake.

When these issues came up, you most likely put things on the back burner and failed to make some payments on certain bills. Changing your habits will help you avoid problems in the future.

For those who got here by mistake or by bad spending habits, it is time to come up with some solutions and a plan of action to make sure this will not happen again.

Have You Overspent?

In Chapter 1, we asked this same question. Have you overspent? We gave some examples of some extras you may be used to and discussed the possibility that you are not being a smart consumer.

Spend Less on Groceries

You will probably find your biggest expense outside of your rent or mortgage and utilities is groceries. This is a necessary evil of life; no one can cut back on groceries. Do not be lulled by the easy but expensive habit of eating out. While it saves you on cooking, it costs more, and is probably less healthy.

You and your family must eat, must have personal grooming items, and need household cleaning supplies, and your pets, if you have them, need food as well.

There is no way around this, but here are some tips for becoming a frugal shopper at the supermarket:

GROCERY TIP # 1: SHOP AT DIFFERENT STORES

If you live in an area with plenty of grocery stores, shop for the best deals. Scour the sales papers for the different grocery chains in the area and see who has the better deals. Then, if prices dictate, go to one place for some of your items and to another for others.

Another approach could be to shop as though there are no supermarkets. For example, for your meat, head to the local meat market. For your produce, find a farmer's market or a fruit shop. For frozen items, you may want to th joining one of the warehouse clubs, like Sam Costco; they are usually cheaper for frozen iter you get so much more. For cleaning supplies a items, try discount stores, such as Big Lots, Dollar General, or Family Dollar. For dairy and groceries, the supermarket will work. Only take this course of action if these stores are in the general vicinity of your home. Otherwise, you will just be taking all the savings you have achieved from smart shopping and letting it trickle through your gas tank because of the high gas prices.

If you still like the convenience of getting everything in one trip, or if you do not have all the store options listed above in your area, try a mom and pop store. A privately owned store, or a chain with only a few locations, may be cheaper than the big supermarket chains in your area.

Another option for people who shop for groceries as a family or a couple is to split up and go to different stores. Take two copies of the list and compare prices via cell phone. That is, of course, if you have a good cell phone contract so a 30-60 minute phone call will not cost you too much.

GROCERY TIP #2: MAKE A LIST AND STICK TO IT

Look through your cabinets, fridge, and freezer to see exactly what you need. Do not deviate from that list. Another way to make a list is to sit down and figure out what you want for dinner for the next week and only buy the items on this list. This will help prevent you from having to go to the store each night to get things for dinner, in which case you may grab some impulse items. Impulse items are a good lead-in to the next tip.

GROCERY TIP #3: DO NOT GO TO THE STORE HUNGRY

is the number one way to put you over your grocery

budget. You need to eat before heading out to buy food. It is simple; when you are hungry, everything looks delicious in the grocery store. You will see something you would never eat, like beef livers or sardines, and because your stomach is growling, you can actually imagine yourself sitting down and eating them. These items will never be eaten and will claim residence in your kitchen until they spoil.

GROCERY TIP #4: BUY GENERIC BRANDS

We talked about this in Chapter 1, and we can not stress enough the importance of knowing that the store brands are just as good as the name brands. Wash the thought out of your head that the store brands are inferior. If there is one thing our government does well it is to safeguard our food through the Food and Drug Administration (FDA). The FDA puts generics under the same scrutiny that name brands, such as Del Monte, Campbell's, and Heinz, are subjected to. You may expect the difference to be about $.50 to $1. This may not seem like much, but when you buy $200 to $300 worth of groceries each month, the savings add up.

GROCERY TIP #5: USE COUPONS

Using coupons may seem like a relic of a bygone area when only the people who lived through the Depression knew the value of saving $0.25 on a can of spinach. With supermarket savings club cards, they tell you that you do not need coupons, that simply having the card will take care of it, but that is only for the in-store specials. Manufactures still send coupons through the mail or send them in your local newspaper. There are also growing Web sites specializing in coupons, such as **www.smartsource. com**. Another Internet option for obtaining coupons are message boards, which let consumers tell each other of places to find good coupons and even to trade coupons. A good example of this is found at **coupons.meetup.com/boards**. If you have a coupon for $0.30 cents off of SPAM and would never eat SPAM, do not just throw the coupon away. Believe us when we tell you there are people out there who love SPAM and would love a coupon for their favorite ham hybrid product. Maybe you can trade it for a coupon for something you love.

Research Ways to Save on Housing Costs

Do not pay more than you have to on utilities. The simplest thing you can do is to take mom's advice from childhood and shut the light off in a room you are leaving. Turn the facet off when you shave or brush your teeth. Do not take hour-long showers. Sure, they feel great, but think of all the wasted water shooting down the drain and adding to your bills. When watching television in the evenings, shut the lights off; you do not see lights on in theaters during the movie. Install motion detectors or light sensors on your outdoor light fixtures, because you might forget to turn them off in the daylight from time to time.

The Internet is a good resource of detailed tips for saving on your utilities. Some good sites are **www.eere.energy.gov/consumer/tips**, which is the U.S. Department of Energy Web site, and **www.fivecentnickel.com**, which, in addition to utilities, provides ideas for saving on other necessities.

If Internet access is a problem for you, try your local library. They will have many books about saving on everything from groceries and utilities to home improvement projects and buying a car. We went over the main drains on your income in the last few sections, but you will have to use your good sense you achieved through bankruptcy to help you navigate the other expenses in your life.

Do Not Make Frivolous, Unnecessary Purchases

You do not need every cable channel, the entire luxury package in a new car, season tickets to all the local sports teams, every new handheld technology, the cell phone with all the extras, the most extravagant wardrobe of all your friends, that vacation home, or toys, such as boats, motorcycles, RVs, ATVs, jet skis, or snow mobiles. These are luxuries. You have to remember where you have been and where you want to go in the future. Picking up one or a few of the above items after bankruptcy may put you back in the same place you were pre-filing, or worse.

If you continue to build your credit, spend your money smartly, and sacrifice, you may one day be in the situation where you can pick up some of those toys.

In the Introduction of the book, we discussed famous people who struggled and then achieved unimagined success after their bankruptcy. They did not do this by going back to their old ways. They learned lessons from bankruptcy to help them become a success. Do not threaten your future by resuming your old spending habits.

Seeking Help for Your Spending Habits

Even if you know you should not be spending the way you are, but you continue to do so, there is help out there for you.

Everyone has heard of Alcoholics Anonymous and their 12-Step Program. This same treatment that has helped so many people quit drinking is also available to people who constantly overspend and always find themselves in debt. The program is called Debtors Anonymous.

Debtors Anonymous' mission statement is as follows:

Debtors Anonymous is a fellowship of men and women who share their experience, strength and hope with each other that they may solve their common problem and help others to recover from compulsive debting.

The only requirement for membership is a desire to stop incurring unsecured debt. There are no dues or fees for D.A. membership; we are self-supporting through our own contributions.

D.A. is not allied with any sect, denomination, politics, organization or institution; does not wish to engage in any controversy; neither endorses nor opposes any causes.

Our primary purpose is to stop debting one day at a time and to help other compulsive debtors to stop incurring unsecured debt.

For more information, go to their Web site, www. debtorsanonymous.org, where you can see whether you need this program with a questionnaire on your spending habits and signs that you are a compulsive spender. You may also call toll free at 1-800-421-2383.

CHAPTER 13

Beginning to Pay Things on Your Own Again & Coming Up with a Workable Budget

"Some couples go over their budgets very carefully every month; others just go over them."
– Sally Poplin, Personal Financer

The biggest shock after being discharged from a Chapter 13 case is the fact that you are now solely responsible for the payments of all your debts, including your mortgage payment, car note (if it survived the discharge), and any debts that were not entitled to a discharge. You have been (or should have been) maintaining all your daily, weekly, and monthly obligations throughout the bankruptcy. You are quite used to using your excess income for paying utilities, filling up the cars with gas, buying groceries, and perhaps buying lunches at work or a cup of coffee on the drive in to work every morning.

Now that you do not have that payment to the trustee, your excess income has increased. Do not make the mistake of thinking that you can know live lavishly again. The reason you have more money in your pocket is because you no longer have funds directly taken out of your check to go to the trustee. If you spend that money on frivolous things, your mortgage will once again be behind, and you will once again find yourself in trouble.

When Will I Know it is Time to Make My Own Mortgage Payment?

This does not always synch up to your exact discharge date. In other words, upon receiving a discharge order, you probably have had one or two mortgage payments come due.

Trustee Letter Ceasing Mortgage Payment

Keep a watchful eye on your mailbox as you approach your discharge. Your trustee will send you a letter telling you the trustee will no longer be paying your mortgage payment and that you will have to start making your own payments. The letter may tell you what date the trustee made the last payment. Make sure to keep this letter for your records in the unlikely event that the mortgage company says the payment for that month was not made.

Wage Release Letter

At this point, if you are sending your payments in directly, you will no longer be required to remit plan payments to the trustee. If your employee automatically sends the payment to the trustee, this will stop. The trustee will send what is called a "wage release letter" to your employer. A copy of this letter will most likely be sent to you as well. Once again, keep this letter for your records just in case your employer takes payments out when they are not supposed to after the letter.

Give it a little time for the letter to work before you start pestering your employer or the trustee, but probably no more than a week. For example, if the letter is sent out from the trustee's office on a Tuesday and it is received in your employer's mail on Thursday; it will more than likely be impossible for the wage deduction to stop for this week, unless you have a very small workplace. If you are paid on a Friday, chances are good the payroll is done on a Thursday, and it will be too late to stop the wage deduction for this week.

Fear not, this money will not be lost. The trustee will recognize this money coming in after they sent the wage release letter and the pay your own mortgage letter and will refund the money back to you. Also, if the trustee realizes the employer is continuing to send payments to them after the wage release letter, they will continue to contact the employer until it has stopped.

Steps for Creating a Budget

First Step: Commit to Following the Budget

The first step to creating a budget is committing to it. It is pointless to take the time to create a budget and make the numbers work, while in the back of your mind, knowing you will not stick to it.

You must understand the importance of creating, implementing, and following the budget – especially if you have a family. You must sell the idea of living on a budget, and the sacrifices that come with that, to your entire family. If you do not believe in the budget, you will not be successful in selling it to other members of the household.

Second Step: Make Sure Everyone is Onboard

If you live on your own, creating a budget will be relatively easy, but if you have a family, it would be advisable to meet as a family and discuss the budget.

In your meeting, you can possibly discuss these topics:

- Make sure they all understand the importance of the budget. Tell your family it will be tough for a while, but no tougher than before or during the bankruptcy. You can tell them that if they sacrifice now, it will help rebuild the family's credit standing, and in time, good things will happen.

- Ask them for suggestions and listen to their questions, comments, and concerns. Ask them for a list of things they can not live without, in order of importance, and if there is money left over on the budget, let them have one or two items off their lists.

- Smaller children may understand, but teenagers may be a tougher sell. Do not get angry and yell if your child is less than happy about the sacrifices they may have to make. Once again, tell them of the importance of never having to go through bankruptcy again.

- Promise incentives. If you have built a little bit of

savings into your budget, take a little out of that and earmark it for a monthly "family night out." Take them to a baseball game or a water park in the summer, or to a movie or other fun indoor activity in the colder months.

- Thank them for sacrificing. Tell them that you are a family and, as such, are in this together. Tell them how much you appreciate their sacrifices and remind them better times are looming on the horizon.

Third Step: Write Down Your Daily Expenses

By creating your budget this way, you technically are not making a budget until the following month. That is because this will help you see what you spend money on every day.

Create a sheet of paper that lists the date, what you are spending money on, and how much it costs. Then total it up and list a daily total. Give a sheet to each member of the household, and tell them to write down everything they spend money on from gas in their car to the $0.30 package of gum they bought.

By doing it this way, you will also notice that you are less likely to buy something frivolously and an expensive item that is unnecessary because you have to document it.

You will want to include your daily purchases as well as your bills. So potentially, if you pay your bills at the beginning of the month, the first of the month total for the day may be very high.

Let us bring back our friends, the Johnsons, who we put through the rigors of the Means Test a while back.

Here is an example of their daily expenses for the first of the month:

JIM JOHNSON – DAILY EXPENSES (4/1)	
Item	**Cost**
Morning Newspaper	$0.50
Coffee	$2.25
Lunch	$7.38
Gas	$40
Daily Total	$50.13
JUDY JOHNSON – DAILY EXPENSES (4/1)	
Item	**Cost**
Gas	$35
Coffee	$2.70
Lunch	$5.28
Haircut	$25
Mortgage	$1,200
Utilities	$375
Cable/Internet	$120
Cell Phones	$130
Daily Total	$1,892.98
JACK JOHNSON (SON – 10 YEARS OLD) – DAILY EXPENSES (4/1)	
Item	**Cost**
Gatorade	$1.99
Bagel	$2.50
School	$4.50
Slurpee	$1.29
Video Game	$53.99
Daily Total	$64.27

JILL JOHNSON (DAUGHTER – 3 YEARS OLD) – DAILY EXPENSES (4/1)	
Item	Cost
Juice	$4.99
Money for lunch	$3
Day care tuition	$400
Daily Total	$407.99

Fourth Step: Analyze Data

At the end of a 30-day period, gather up everyone's receipts and total them up. Then analyze the data to see whether you or a member of the family is spending too much. Since listing four people's spending for 30 months would take up too many pages and kill too many trees, we will just dissect the budget for the date shown, April 1.

You may be wondering why the fifth member of the Johnson household, Jim's mom, was not included. Jim's mom resided in the household and paid rent. Remember, though, that she has her own income and expenses, and as such, did not figure into any of the expense calculations we did for the family in the Means Test in Chapter 6.

If you notice, Judy has all the mortgage and utilities on her expense sheet. This is because she deals with the bills in the home. You will expect Judy's (or anyone else's, for that matter) expenses to not approach that level again for the rest of the month, since now all the monthly bills have been paid.

You may also notice that both Jim and Judy filled up their cars. They usually fill up once per week each, unless they have to drive more than usual. Judy got a haircut "today."

On average, the family gets haircuts once a month, except for young Jill. So you can expect three members of the family to have a haircut expense on one of their sheets.

You will see that Jack bought a video game for $53.99 ($49.99 + 8 percent tax). He received permission from his parents to buy this game for a good report card. This is obviously not an everyday purchase, and more than likely, it will not be seen again in the month.

Finally, Jill needed juice for the house and is required to take $3 to daycare each day for a hot lunch. Since it is the first of the month, Judy took in a check for the daycare costs, $400, for the month. Since Jill is so young and sometimes stays home with her grandmother, many days, her expenses are at $0, as are Jack's on the weekends.

Your expenses will fluctuate between the weekdays and weekends, so be prepared for the higher or lower expenses you have on the weekends.

Just by analyzing this one day, assumptions can be made. The family is not overspending too much, but some sacrifices can be made. Jack could go without the video game, but Jim and Judy are adamant about giving positive reinforcement. Both adults buy coffee on their way into work in the morning. This could be stamped out by buying coffee and travel mugs and making their own coffee at home. A can of coffee can seem expensive at between $6 and $10, depending on the size, but a couple of times of taking coffee from home will more than make up for the cost of one cup of coffee from various coffee houses or donut shops everyday. Also, it appears Jack buys Gatorade and a bagel for breakfast. This can get pricey (not to mention unhealthy). Maybe a deal could be worked out with Jim's mom to make breakfast for the kids before school, if Jim or Judy do not have time to do it, for a break on her rent. Another way to save money is to "brownbag" it to work, school, and daycare. Take some time in the evenings to make lunches, and you will save more money than you realize.

Fifth (and Final) Step: Come Up With a Monthly Budget

Now take all the information you have come up with, the concessions you have made, and make your monthly budget.

Work hard to stay within the confines of the budget. Obviously, things happen from time to time that may make you go over your budget for the month, but most months, you should be fine.

Try to set aside as much as you can. Even $100 each month can add up after a while. This savings will provide you with a parachute if things go south again.

If you stay on your budget, save as much as you can, learn how to be a smart consumer, and learn how to obtain credit in your post-bankruptcy life (as we will discuss about in the next and final chapter), the credit problems and the bankruptcy will be a distant, but important, memory, and you will be able to get on with your life.

As we move to the final chapter, let us bid adieu to our serviceable family, the Johnsons.

CHAPTER 14

Obtaining and Repairing Your Credit Post-Bankruptcy

"Credit is a system whereby a person who can not pay gets another person who can not pay to guarantee that he can pay."
– Charles Dickens, Famous British Novelist

Credit may have hurt you in the past, but it is a necessary thing. If you have gotten to this point, you thoroughly understand that your credit will take a hit for a couple of years after your discharge from bankruptcy. You know, though, that as we have said before, having difficulty obtaining credit for a few years post-discharge is much better than having several unpaid debts on your credit report for much longer than the affects are felt after a bankruptcy.

As we close this book about bankruptcy, we want to stress the importance of continuing to clean up your credit. Do not just rest on your laurels after bankruptcy. You have been proactive all along in this process. Take a minute to look back at the process you have been through.

You carefully looked at all your options, decided to file for bankruptcy, and chose which the chapter fit you best. You made sure to attend all your hearings. You paid attention to all mailings from the court or trustee to make sure you did not miss anything required of you. You made all your payments timely (if in a Chapter 13) and did everything required of you in your case.

You successfully received a discharge, and you should feel accomplished. Many people file for bankruptcy, but not all of them receive a discharge. Now is not the time to relax and let the world go by. Celebrate (frugally of course), but then it is time to go back to work.

Pull Your Credit Report Once Again

The first step is to do something you already did, months (in a Chapter 7) or years (in a Chapter 13) before, and that is to check your credit report once again.

Chances are good, if you have filed for a Chapter 13, that you have not accessed your credit report in a number of years, so you will be entitled to your yearly free report. Refer back to Chapter 3 of this book to see how you can obtain your credit report.

If you have filed for a Chapter 7, you will likely have to pay for your credit report since you are accessing it twice in a twelve month period, but as we stated in Chapter 3, there is only a nominal fee.

Make sure you check that all the information listed is correct by using the criteria we set forth in Chapter 3. This time, you will need to make sure all the debts that were eliminated or paid in full during the bankruptcy are properly notated as such. It should say something along the lines of, "discharged in bankruptcy" for a Chapter 7, or "paid through bankruptcy" for a Chapter 13. If you do not see this, it should raise some red flags.

As we discussed in Chapter 3, credit reports are notoriously erroneous. With the incredible number of filings and the confusion before the change over to the new code in October 2005, many additional mistakes were made with creditors reporting wrong information. Be very diligent in reviewing your credit report.

First, make sure this was a dischargeable debt, meaning it was not a domestic support obligation, recent tax obligation, or a student loan. Next, make sure the creditor received proper notice.

Refer back to the original credit report you pulled pre-bankruptcy. You should keep all your bankruptcy documents for at least ten years, when the bankruptcy will be taken off your record for good. In your records, you should have kept your original credit report (if your attorney wanted to keep it, you should have made a copy). This way, you can check back and make sure this creditor was properly noticed on your Matrix. If they were on your credit report pre-bankruptcy, it stands to reason they were noticed out, since the attorney likely used your credit report when listing your creditors so the court could provide notice of the bankruptcy.

If everything seems to have been noticed correctly, and these debts are eligible for a discharge, you will need to address this situation immediately. You want to make sure everything on your credit report, except for the bankruptcy, is seen by potential creditors as a positive, meaning closed accounts that have been paid in full. Seeing several open accounts will possibly make a creditor think you have started charging up credit cards and creating other debt, and they may deny you credit.

To challenge something on your credit report, you must write to the credit reporting agency that issued the report. There will be a form for the challenging of the report sent along with the report itself. As we discussed in Chapter 3, there are several ways of submitting it.

This time, since you are challenging the report on the basis of a debt that should have gone away upon discharge from the bankruptcy, you need to include some specific information and documents to back up your claim.

This information is:

- A copy of the discharge order you received from the court. Do not send the original; keep that for your records.

- Copies of your schedules, particularly the ones that list your creditors. You can send them all, but make sure at least Schedules D, E, F, and G are sent.

- Send copies of your identification: driver's license and social security card.

- Additional proof of your current address, such as a utility bill.

You should receive a response within 30 to 45 days. If you

are certain the debt was entitled to a discharge, then with the evidence you have provided, the credit report will be updated.

Obtain a Secured Credit Card

There is a "safe" credit card you can obtain and not risk falling back into the world of overspending and bankruptcy. This card is referred to as a "secured" credit card.

How It Works

A secured card requires a cash collateral deposit that becomes the credit line for that account. You spend only what you put in; for example, if you put $300 in the account, you can only charge up to $300. If you want additional credit on the card, you will add money to it. This way, you are not running up bills for money you do not have, you simply pay as you go.

Having some sort of credit card is a must for two reasons, and having a secured credit card gives you piece of mind to know you can not overcharge yourself back into debt.

Advantages of a Secured Credit Card

Having a Credit Card is a Necessity

One reason for having a credit card these days is that, frankly, society dictates that you have one. Try renting a car on vacation or for business purposes without a credit card. It is very difficult, and in many cases, impossible.

Try renting a hotel room without a credit card. You can do it, but usually the hotel wants a credit card number to hold a set amount on your card until you checkout. If you give them the okay to run the credit card, they will refund the hold minus your room charges. If you do not have a credit card but want to pay cash, in many cases, the hotel will ask for the amount of money they would hold on your credit card in cash. The hold can be very costly, sometimes in the hundreds of dollars. If you are on a trip, that takes away a large chunk of your spending and meal money.

If you want to book a flight in advanced without a credit card, be prepared to drive to the airport or a travel agency to book your reservations face to face in order to pay cash. If you choose this route, you will have to successfully find a travel agency. These days with the emergence of Internet travel sites such as Expedia and Travelocity, which require credit cards, traditional travel agents are becoming increasingly tough to find.

Finally, an increasing number of specialty stores and even supermarkets have stopped taking checks. With the growth of bank-issued debit cards with the Visa or MasterCard logo on the card, checks have become increasingly obsolete. If you do not have one of these, be prepared to carry cash at all times.

You can use one of those debit cards as a stand-in for a credit card for many of the above instances, but if you live paycheck to paycheck, you may not have enough money for the hold hotels, and sometimes car rental companies, put on your card. Also, this does nothing to help you rebuild your credit.

Rebuild Your Credit

This is the second reason you want a secured credit card. It looks good on your credit report. Believe it or not, people who have no credit have equally poor credit scores as people who have bad credit. The reason being is that if someone has no credit, no one knows how they will handle credit if and when they obtain some.

If you merely check your credit report, verify that it is correct, and do nothing to try to obtain credit, your credit score will recover slowly over the years after your bankruptcy discharge, but the fact that you have had no credit whatsoever since the filing of the bankruptcy will reflect negatively on you.

Regular, or "unsecured," Credit Cards or "Secured" Credit Cards

You do not have to go the secured route, if you would rather dive back into the regular credit card world. You probably will not be approved for a regular, or an unsecured, credit card right away, but eventually, you will be. If you do gain approval, be prepared to crane your head skyward for that interest rate.

In Chapter 11, we talked about all the ridiculous offers you will get from credit card companies for pre-approved cards. You could always take up the credit companies on their offers after your discharge and accept these pre-approved cards. The interest rate will be out of this world, and if the debt ceiling is high, the temptation will always be there. If you commit to paying off the balance every month, then this may work for you. The credit card company will report your account in good standing, and your credit score will gradually increase, but with these cards, you are one impulse item from being pushed back into debt.

The secured card allows you to have a source of emergency money and allows you to easily book a flight, hold a hotel room, or rent a car. The secured card will report your account in good standing, you will not have an interest rate, and you will not have the temptation of a seemingly endless debt ceiling. It is the best case scenario.

Disadvantages of Using Secured Credit Cards

The first disadvantage of secured cards is that you may have to shop around a bit to find them. If you belong to a credit union, ask whether they have them available for their customers. Many do at lower annual fees than you would find through name brand credit card companies, or "the big boys," such as Discover or MBNA.

If you do not belong to a credit union, or yours does not offer this type of card, you may have to shop around through the "big boys." These companies have higher interest rates and an annual charge, which means you may have to put, say, $560 into an account to have a $500 credit line.

The fees are the second disadvantage. Some of the bigger companies and many credit unions, albeit at a lower rate, will debit money for a "service fee" if you have the credit card over a long period of time.

As with everything, be sure to read everything thoroughly, even if it means buying a magnifying glass at the dollar store to read the fine print. You do not want to be hit with any charges and see your money whittle away in a matter of months.

To start shopping around for the right card for you, go to **www.bankrate.com** for an extensive list of secured credit card providers.

Be Sure to Have Bank Accounts

You may have lost all faith in banks when in the height of your troubles; pre-bankruptcy your "friendly neighborhood bank" heaped charges upon charges on an already overdrawn, or nearly overdrawn, bank account. The natural feeling after this is to abandon your bank accounts and pay your bills in cash.

Even though you are angry, this is not the right approach. For one thing, not every bill is paid in cash, so you will need money orders, which cost money themselves. You may have trouble cashing your payroll check. You will be able to cash it at the bank that is issuing it, but you will probably be charged a fee if you do not have a bank account at this bank. Then, in the unlikely event that your residence is broken into, in addition to the shock of losing your personal items, you will also be utterly broke, as your savings will have been stolen.

We all know bank fees are too high, but like paying $3 a gallon for gas, they are a necessity in life. The alternatives are just too inconvenient.

Finally, when looking for credit, the lenders will look to see whether you have open bank accounts. If you do not, it will concern them that you have no way of paying your bills.

Also, be sure not to bounce checks in your checking account because that will be reported on your credit report.

Ask for Information to be Added to Your Credit Report

Certain things not credit related will go toward your favor if you can get them added to your credit report.

Send a letter to the credit bureau and ask them to add the following if they apply to you:

- **Your current employer** (and former employer if you have recently changed jobs). This will show the creditor stability in your income. Be careful with this, though; if you have non-discharged debts, the creditor may use this information to garnish your wages, but chances are, if this was the same employer you had during your bankruptcy, they will already have this address.

- **Your current address,** if you own it (and former address if you have been at your current address for two years or less).

- **Telephone number.** We are all reluctant to give this out, but if a creditor can not verify a phone number, they are not likely to give credit.

- **Social security number** for identification purposes.

The credit bureau is not obligated to add this information, but will most likely do so.

One additional item that can be added to a credit report is something that people usually do not know about, and even if they do, fail to use. Your credit report is required to print a short paragraph in your own words that you can write stating why you fell into bankruptcy.

This is particularly handy for someone who was always a smart consumer, always paid their bills on time, or never overspent and was pushed into bankruptcy because of an illness or other catastrophe. You can explain this, and a creditor looking to give you credit will be able to see that you filed bankruptcy by no fault of your own. Without this paragraph, the creditor would not know the circumstances behind the bankruptcy.

Even for the individuals who had to file for bankruptcy because of irresponsible spending, it may serve you well to write something like this:

"I reached a point in my life where my debt overwhelmed me and I was unable to meet my commitments. After a great deal of research and consultation with many people, I decided that bankruptcy was the best option for me at that time. I truly believe I have learned an incredible and indelible life lesson and will never make the same mistake again."

If you filed for a Chapter 13, you can use the above, but somewhere in the passage, put in something like the following:

"I committed whole heartedly to my bankruptcy. I never

missed a payment, I complied with every order of my case, I sent in all the tax refunds that I was bound to remit, and I was able to offer 100 percent payment to all my creditors."

If not a 100 percent plan, include something like this:

"...while I was unable to pay off all my unsecured creditors in full, I made sure they got as much as I could possibly afford by my filing of a Chapter 13, instead of a Chapter 7, in which they would have received nothing. It was important for me to try to pay back what I could."

Creditors are not bound to accept any of this, but you will have a better chance of obtaining credit than if you did not take advantage of this opportunity.

Be Weary of Credit Relief Companies

Anyone who has had a sick day and watched awful daytime television will recognize the equally awful daytime television commercials for credit relief agencies. You will also see these offers coming in the mail or on your phone if you do not hang up quick enough.

They may promise to erase your bad credit, bankruptcies, or past credit indiscretions.

No one can erase anything off of a credit report. The only thing that can make something vanish off of a credit report is time. All items, good and bad, disappear off of a credit report over time. No organization can make these items disappear faster.

How Can I Obtain a Mortgage or a Car Loan Just After Bankruptcy?

Everything we have described above is the way to make this easy, but these steps are meant to be completed over a period of time. Many bankruptcy experts say that you will see some normalization of your credit options about two years after your discharge. Your options will increase and the interest rates will decline (somewhat).

Two years is a long time, particularly if your housing situation is not certain (i.e., renting) or you have a car lease that is expiring within two years. You may think it is impossible to get credit during this time, and while it is difficult and takes plenty of time and patience for investigation and shopping around, it is not as hard as you might think.

You have seen the mailings you have received for credit cards, so you know there are lenders out there. Yes, getting a car loan and a mortgage will be a little tougher because some creditors will draw the line and make it policy to not deal with people just out of bankruptcy, but that may work in your benefit because that is one less creditor to research.

There is no way around it; you will have to pay a high interest rate. The interest rate is basically a trade-off with the creditor. You are paying more for their issuing of the loan; in other words, you have to pay more because there is a greater possibility you will not pay the entire amount over time.

The bottom line is that you will have to do some work to get credit or loans after your bankruptcy is discharged, and if you can all wait for that invisible two-year window to close, you will have many more options available for you, but if you have to have a new car or house right now, you will probably be able to get it.

Look at it this way. We have talked in depth about how you are not alone in filing for bankruptcy. For every one person who files for bankruptcy, there are many more who do not and deal with their debts other ways. Their credit is shot as well. This means many Americans are in credit dire straights, and the creditor is in business to issue credit and loans, so chances are, people with bad credit will be getting a loan.

Conclusion

"Bankruptcy"

To many, that is a dirty word.

You may remember we started this book this exact same way.

You may have started this process having that exact same sentiment about bankruptcy. Now that you have lived it for a few months or years, you know it is not "dirty." In fact, it is just the opposite. It is a fresh start.

It is up to you to correct the people who still think this way. Tell them that bankruptcy may happen to them one day because no one is perfect.

Chances are good that bumps in the road will happen along the path of life. The important thing is how those bumps will affect you.

If you did nothing to address your debts, if you sat staring at the phone for years hoping you could go one day without a creditor calling or discovering your new phone number or address, then you were incapacitated by that bump in the road called debt.

If you filed for bankruptcy or found better options, then you hit that bump in stride, because nothing is going to get in the way of you, your family, and your life. You decided you wanted to do something about your problem and make it go away so you could get on with your life.

Where you go from here is up to you.

If you have read this book from cover to cover, chances are, you have read other books, searched the Internet, and done plenty of other research to find out which is the best course of action for you. You may have gotten attached to all your reference materials, because when you had a question, all you had to do was flip open the book and there was the answer.

For some who were so dependent on a book, it is tough to start to live life and field the daily circumstances that come up on their own with no point of reference to help them.

If you have come this far in your bankruptcy and you are committed to a fresh start, then nothing can keep you down.

Our hope is you can put this book on a shelf and let it get dusty because that will mean you never had to file for bankruptcy again. If someday you have to file again, come back and we will refresh your memory about the process.

Have faith in yourself and you will do well.

Please use the Case Studies section of this book, which is coming up next. Each Case Study is written by individuals on the front lines of the bankruptcy community, or people in the financial world. They will have suggestions on how to file for bankruptcy, the options instead of bankruptcy, what to do after bankruptcy, how to save money, and how to rebuild you credit. Please enjoy these writings; you can learn much from these learned people.

As we leave you, the author would like to share with you one of his favorite stories from his youth.

It is from the late author Shel Silverstein. You most likely have heard of Shel and his collections of stories in books titled, Where the Sidewalk Ends and A Light in the Attic, or his stand alone books, such as The Giving Tree.

We have tried to make each quote in this book relate to some part of the bankruptcy process. This piece has nothing to do with any of that. What it does relate to is living life to the fullest before it is too late.

Debtors being released from bankruptcy are akin to children in the way that they have a fresh, innocent start awaiting them. Do not spoil it.

Without further ado, we close the book with a hearty "good luck" and the words of the immortal Shel Silverstein and his poem, "The Folks Inside."

The Folks Inside
By Shel Silverstein

"Inside you, boy,

There's an old man sleepin'

Dreamin,' waitin' for his chance.

Inside you, girl,

There's an old lady dozin,'

Wantin' to show you a slower dance.

So keep on playin,'

Keep on runnin,'

Keep on jumpin,' till the day

That those old folks

Down inside you

Wake up. . . and come out to play."

Case Studies

CASE STUDY #1: JANET BENEDETTI

Case Administrator
Office of the Chapter 13 Trustee-Krispen S. Carroll
Detroit, Michigan

I have had quite a great deal of experience in the bankruptcy community. I have been doing bankruptcy work for over 20 years. I worked for nine years with a creditor doing collections, foreclosures and bankruptcies, a few years with a debtor attorney and eleven years with The Office of the Standing Chapter 13 Trustee.

I learned the terminology and the basics of Chapters 7 and 13 at a very large mortgage company, who serviced loans for Freddie Mac, Fannie Mae and other lesser known insurers. Any creditor's focus, of course, is "Are we getting paid?" If no payments are being received, the creditor will start legal action to try to collect its money. A mortgage company is particularly aggressive in order to protect its insurers and investors, especially with the housing situation being what it is today. A timely bankruptcy can stop a foreclosure, but the mortgage company can take additional legal action by motioning the Court to remove or "lift" the bankruptcy stay. Generally speaking, mortgage payments still need to be paid in order to save the home. All the costs incurred by the mortgage company in its collection and foreclosure efforts are passed on to the debtor.

CASE STUDY #1: JANET BENEDETTI

As legal assistant with a bankruptcy attorney, the focus changes to stopping the creditor from taking any legal action. Often, there is an urgency to halt a foreclosure on a home, or to stop creditors from garnisheeing a paycheck. The attorney needs to act fast to ascertain the debtor's complete financial picture: employment information; income(s) and expenses; assets and liabilities; household size; tax return information. The various forms and schedules need to be prepared, signed, and timely filed at the Bankruptcy Court. The debtor also needs to obtain a credit counseling certificate from a certified agency, a new twist under BAPCCA laws. In addition to the attorney's fee, there are court fees for filing the documents, and there are fees for credit counseling services. The attorney should disclose these fees to the debtor and discuss method of payment.   The attorney fee is usually factored into the Chapter 13 plan, more costly than a Chapter 7, because 13's are more complicated. Bookkeeping is usually done in house, most likely by one of the attorneys. The attorney time, the employee time, the copying costs, the court filing fees, and the postage costs are all expenses that can be passed on to the debtor.

The Trustee, a different entity from the Bankruptcy court, takes the position of a fiduciary, the one who holds property or money in trust. The duties of the Chapter 13 Trustee begin as soon as the case is electronically forwarded by the court. Any documents that pertain to or affect a Chapter 13 plan are examined for errors and inconsistencies as well as adherence to the Federal Bankruptcy rules. The Trustee evaluates the financial plan that is put forth and makes a determination of feasibility of a plan. All documents that are filed during the life of the plan are reviewed: amendments, motions, applications, objections, proofs of claims, etc. The case is monitored throughout the life of the plan and if all terms are met, the Trustee progresses the case to discharge. The Trustee does not give legal advice, to the consternation of many Pro Se debtors, but the Trustee is mindful of the best interests of both the debtor and the creditor. The Trusteeship plays a crucial role in the bankruptcy process.

My advice for people thinking of representing themselves in bankruptcy would be to "think again." For some people the bankruptcy process can be very invasive and they may be embarrassed of their situation. For others, it's just a practical issue. But, they all want to protect whatever assets they have. A good bankruptcy attorney is better equipped to make sure that happens.

CASE STUDY #1: JANET BENEDETTI

Some people may try to file In Pro Per after a free consultation with an attorney, but not many leave this first meeting armed with the knowledge needed to represent themselves. There is just too much pertinent information that cannot be learned from a "how to" book or by downloading forms from the internet. A Pro Se debtor can save some money, but for the person who is serious about straightening out their finances, there could be some serious consequences. Any number of things could happen during the 3 to 5 year term of a Chapter 13 bankruptcy plan. Family emergencies such as the loss of a job, birth of a baby, death in the family, or need of transportation or home repairs, can cause additional financial hardship as well as emotional turmoil. A bankruptcy attorney can counsel the debtor through the process of modifying the terms of the bankruptcy plan, or adjusting the payment obligations or even obtaining new credit. Added services may mean added fees, but just the fact that all documents are now electronically filed may be enough to discourage some from filing Pro Se. Not too many Pro Se cases in a Chapter 13 case actually get confirmed or proceed to discharge without an attorney's help. But it has happened. Those of us in the business would probably not represent themselves if faced with a bankruptcy.

Try to find a reputable attorney, one who is proficient in filing bankruptcies. Don't shop for bargains, the fees for filing a case are generally the same across the board. Be honest to your attorney (and to yourself) about your financial situation. If you don't give a true picture of your circumstances, your bankruptcy could fail and may end up costing more in the long run, monetarily and otherwise. Ask a lot of questions about the process and how it affects you and what you can expect during your time in bankruptcy. READ THE PAPERS YOU SIGN. A successful Chapter 7 or Chapter 13 ends with a discharge, not a dismissal.

BAPCPA has created "tighter" regulations with the intention of stopping abuse. There are now more "tests" to pass, so to speak. As a result, the bankruptcy process has become more cumbersome for all the parties involved. Although electronic filing eliminated the need for triplicate copies of all documents, the actual amount of paperwork has grown. The attorney fees have gone up. Court filing fees have increased. There is now an added expense to the debtor for credit counseling courses, one when filing a case and another prior to receiving a discharge. The theory is that debtor

CASE STUDY #1: JANET BENEDETTI

education will prevent future repeat and/or abusive filings. Despite this attempt to stop abuse, however, repeat filings continue, and new filings persist regardless of new regulations and income levels. Understandably, many in the bankruptcy community attribute the rise in fees and costs directly to the added requirements of BAPCPA.

There are many reasons a first case could fail and needs to be re-filed, but "serial filers" usually raise suspicion of abuse. Because filing bankruptcy can be complex for any number of reasons, some cases may need to be re-filed simply due to lack of knowledge of the process. In either case, the general perception is not good. It really depends on the specific reasons a case has failed. The judges are well aware of the facts of a case and they make informed decisions. Some judges appear to be more patient and understanding and won't deny the debtors a second or even a third chance to try for a successful bankruptcy. Others show a lower tolerance and will make the decision to dismiss a case. A judge can also restrain a debtor from filing another case for a set period of time, particularly if signs of abuse are evident.

A Chapter 13 usually requires a 3 to 5 year commitment. Failing to meet the payment obligations pursuant to the bankruptcy plan is the biggest detriment to a successful case. An attorney may be needed to help resolve these issues and could cause the debtor to incur additional attorney fees when they are already struggling to make ends meet.

A discharge is a great thing! Ideally, a successful plan has provided the debtor with a clean slate. The biggest mistake would be repeating the same things that landed them in bankruptcy in the first place. Many find they face repeating the bankruptcy process because they have again fallen behind on the mortgage, have incurred new credit card debt, and are still spending more than they can afford.

It's very basic, really. Spend less than what you earn. If you can't afford it, don't buy it. Cut up the credit cards.

CASE STUDY # 2: SHAWN SHIVNEN M.P.A.

Advanced Placement Economics and
Economics Teacher
Romulus High School
Romulus, Michigan

I feel bankruptcy should not be the first option. It can be a consideration, but people need to seek out the advice of several qualified individuals on their options before taking a drastic action such as bankruptcy.

If you find yourself in financial troubles, talk to someone who handles bankruptcy, but also talk to a few different credit counselors. Every different credit counseling agency handles negotiations differently among credit card companies. So you can pick the one that best matches you.

My initial thought is irresponsible and shortsighted thinking puts a lot of people into bankruptcy these days. Besides initial irresponsibility, I would bet that a lot of people have been severely affected by the increase in adjustable rate mortgages from the refinancing and housing boom. On the other hand, not having the financial literacy or the foresight to limit their potential risk to an adjustable rate mortgage is as much their fault and the reason for their bankruptcy.

Other causes could be poor financial literacy, refusal or unwillingness to make a budget and stick to it, credit card abuse, medical bills or illness. I am sure the causes are many, but usually boil down to either someone not being responsible in their finances or an event happening that causes then to borrow and spend at a pace which they can not sustain over the long run.

My advice to recently discharged bankruptcy debtors would be to live within your means, follow your budget, do not keep a balance on your credit cards, keep money in your savings account and meet with someone who can help you. There are a lot of non profit agencies out there that specialize in helping people in these situations.

CASE STUDY # 2: SHAWN SHIVNEN M.P.A.

Specifically, here is what you can do:

- Make a budget and stay within it. If you can not operate an excel spreadsheet, find someone who can. Knowing your expenses and your income every month is a powerful tool in living within your means.

- Do not buy anything on credit that you can not pay off at the end of your billing cycle.

- Start saving, even if it is a small amount. If times ever get rough again, you will want something to fall back on or get you through the tough times.

- Build your credit back up, pay your bills on time and keep only one credit card with the balance paid off each month.

Live within your budget and your means, whatever has happened in the past means that you can not have the expensive toys or furniture until your financial situation improves. Do not even think about it, just worry about the things you can control.

CASE STUDY # 3: PAT PELC

Former Staff Member of Chapter 13 Trustees
Krispen S. Carroll &
David Ruskin
Detroit, Michigan
Former Mortgage Loan Officer, Vision Mortgage
Southfield, Michigan

I was in the bankruptcy community for seven years at two different trustees' in Detroit. I was a legal assistant in both offices. After leaving the trustees' office, I went on to work in the mortgage business where I helped debtors during and after their bankruptcy obtain credit.

CASE STUDY # 3: PAT PELC

It is very important for a debtor to seek the advice of an attorney. Proceeding on your own is a very bad idea. In all my years working in the bankruptcy field I have never seen a successful Chapter 13 Pro Se case. There are so many steps to a successful bankruptcy that are not easily understood and the debtor's property and home needs to be protected. Debtors are not familiar enough with exemptions, reaffirmation agreements or the process of notification of creditors. All of these issues, procedures and requirements can make or break a bankruptcy case.

Bankruptcy Reform has made it harder and much more difficult for a Debtor to file a Chapter 7 and discharge their unsecured debts with no payback to creditors. Many Debtors who once could have filed a Chapter 7 now have to file a Chapter 13 case and make some form of restitution to unsecured creditors. The Means Test and credit counseling requirements make filing much more complex than pre-2005.

My tips for how a debtor can help make his or her bankruptcy case a success, would be:

- MAKE ALL OF YOUR PAYMENTS ON TIME!! This is absolutely crucial for your post-bankruptcy credit status as well as makes your bankruptcy successful.

- Attend all Court hearings.

- Be proactive in dealing with any notices you may receive in the mail.

- Be honest with your attorney.

In my experience, I have found that when a debtor files multiple cases, either the debtor was not completely honest and forthcoming with their attorney about all aspects of his/her financial situation or debtor failed to honor the commitment made to the bankruptcy case or debtor had an inexperienced or bad attorney.

Generally, and especially in the case of a Debtor who owns a home that

CASE STUDY # 3: PAT PELC

could be subject to a foreclosure, the judge will place a 180 day bar to refilling a case, thus giving the mortgage company time to complete the foreclosure process.

I have seen debtors make numerous mistakes which have caused their cases to be dismissed. Not making timely payments to the chapter 13 Trustee, failure to attend court hearings and failure to report accurate and truthful income and expenses are some of the most common downfalls of debtors.

In my time in the bankruptcy world and after, in the mortgage industry I have also seen debtors make mistakes after they have received their discharge. This sometimes lands the debtors back to where they were before filing, or worse, back in bankruptcy. One of the most common mistakes is not checking their credit report periodically to insure creditors are accurately reporting and discharging the debts included in the bankruptcy. A second, even more serious mistake is to allow themselves to go back in debt once again. Just remember to live within your means and remember that your bankruptcy was a fresh start.

I have seen debtors post-discharge successfully rebuild their credit in a short period of time. My advice to these debtors would be to get one credit card – a secured credit card. Deposit $200-$500 with this card, use it and pay the balance monthly as required. This will allow the creditor to report a good payment history on your credit report.

Here are other things you can do:

- You can actually help yourself out pre-discharge by maintaining a good payment history to the trustee during your bankruptcy case. Mortgage companies will look at the payment history to the trustee in making a decision on any mortgage financing.

- Pay utility payments on time. This is another criterion that mortgage lenders will look at before extending credit either during or after a bankruptcy.

- Any post-bankruptcy filings debts, such as reaffirmed mortgage or

CASE STUDY # 3: PAT PELC

car payments must be paid, be current and have a good payment history.

If all payment to the bankruptcy were made on time, if the plan was proposed in good faith and completed in a timely manner; many times I have seen debtors with a higher credit score than people who never filed a bankruptcy.

CASE STUDY # 4: ELISSE LOPEZ

Chapter 7 Debtor filed in New York State
Recently filed with her husband and they are
awaiting their discharge

The main reason I filed for a Chapter 7 was because we were unable to obtain health insurance and I became very ill during that time. I had various hospitalizations, surgery and medications. This led to numerous medical bills, totaling over $100,000, which ultimately became impossible to pay. The hospital was unwilling to work with us. We had to choose between paying the medical bills or putting food on the table and keeping a roof over our heads. We chose the latter.

We decided to go for Chapter 7 because it offered the "fresh start" we sought. Also, our attorney advised us to go for chapter 7 because we did not own any properties or have a lot of assets. He stated that Chapter 13 is more appropriate for people who have things of value that they want or need to keep such as homes, cars, property and jewelry.

Bankruptcy was our last option because, quite frankly, it is not something you want to think about. I think that we felt that bankruptcy would mean we had failed at something in our lives. We attempted to work with the hospital for lower payments but they did not offer any reasonable solutions. We researched bankruptcy and realized that the pros outweighed the cons.

We hired an attorney to assist us. In the past we attempted to represent ourselves in an unrelated case and the outcome was not good at all. At that

CASE STUDY # 4: ELISSE LOPEZ

time we decided that ANY legal matter that might come up in the future, we would seek the representation of an attorney.

The overall experience with our attorney was okay. He was very friendly and very understanding. He seemed knowledgeable about bankruptcy laws and everything was filed accordingly. However, he arrived late the day of our 341 meeting and the trustee chewed him out. We thought it was a bit irresponsible of him to arrive late and thought about letting him know we were upset but the trustee took care of it for us. Ever since the pre-discharge debtor online course was completed, he has not communicated with us to keep us posted. We have had to be on top of it.

Our main concern when filing bankruptcy was, of course, our credit and how it would affect us in the future. However, we have never had a problem with living beyond our means with credit cards and we do not own property or have any large payments. Overall we thought it would be better to do it now than later. We have plans to purchase a home next year so we are aware that it will affect us greatly. We read that after two years or so a lot of people are able to get loans. We will cross our fingers and, in the meantime, work on re-establishing our credit.

There WAS a sense of embarrassment in the beginning but we realize that we are not the only ones in this situation. We realized that having the option to file for bankruptcy is something to appreciate. Our thinking is that you never know where you will be tomorrow. Today we are on the bottom, but tomorrow it could be you or you or YOU! Of course, we do not go around announcing the bankruptcy, not because of embarrassment, but because it is no one else's business. If the bankruptcy comes up for a required transaction, like a credit check for renting, loans, etc., we will mention it beforehand to avoid wasting our time or anyone else's. I do not know how many companies file for bankruptcy everyday and no one puts any shame on them. Therefore, we do not feel ashamed either.

We did not get into debt because of overspending so managing budgets and credit is not something we needed to learn. However, there is ALWAYS room for improvement so we will try to use credit as little as possible after our discharge. We also are more aware of due dates and have become more

CASE STUDY # 4: ELISSE LOPEZ

organized to avoid sending in payments late. We have medical insurance now, so hopefully we will not have those huge medical debts ever again. One huge change we have made is that we have gotten much more serious about saving. We are working to save up enough to get us by for at least six months should anything unexpected come up. In addition, we are researching options for retirement funds.

I do not know if I would recommend bankruptcy to a friend or family, simply because it is a really personal choice and a decision someone has to make on their own. We have no qualms about sharing our experience if someone asks for advice, but bankruptcy is such a taboo and carries so much shame that a friend or relative may never even tell you they are having financial problems. I suppose it really depends on the relationship you have with someone. If they are close to you, I suppose one could bring up the topic about bankruptcy as an option, but if they are not so close, sometimes you are better off keeping your mouth shut until asked to do otherwise.

CASE STUDY # 5: BRIAN SMALL

Bankruptcy Attorney/Partner
Thav, Gross, Steinway & Bennett P.C.
30150 Telegraph Road, Suite 444
Bingham Farms, Michigan 48025
Bankruptcy@thavgross.com
www.stopcreditorcalls.com
(248) 645-1700

CLASSIFIED CASE STUDIES
directly from the experts

I have been in the bankruptcy field for 18 years. My first two years were as a law clerk in Virginia and the last 16 years have been as an attorney in Michigan. I have also worked for the Office of the United States Trustee and two law firms. I have been the managing partner of my firm's bankruptcy practice for the last six years.

Representing yourself in a bankruptcy (pro se) is generally a bad idea; there is so much risk, with too little reward. Under BAPCPA, there is only one opportunity to file a bankruptcy and receive a Chapter 7 discharge every eight years. A Pro Se debtor may think that they have filled out the petition,

CASE STUDY # 5: BRIAN SMALL

schedules, and statement of financial affairs correctly, however, if they should not have filed a case, for any number of reasons, they lose there opportunity to correct the situation later. If at all possible, hire an attorney. If you can not afford an attorney, seek out the "pro bono" practitioners in your area. I once read that filing a bankruptcy is the one of the most traumatic events that a person can go through. Having an attorney help you through the process is vital, both to be sure it is done right and to be sure that you have someone to guide you through the process. It is not just a matter of filling out paperwork and crossing your fingers. In all my years of bankruptcy, I have seen very few instances of successful Pro Se cases, and those instances were only in very simple Chapter 7 cases. I have never seen a successful Pro Se Chapter 13 case.

In my opinion, BAPCPA has changed bankruptcy in very few ways. A very small percentage of my clients, who would have been a candidate for bankruptcy pre-BAPCPA, have been affected by the change in the law other than the following observation: The biggest impact of BAPCPA upon a debtor is that those individuals who file a Chapter 13 case with income above the IRS "median" must go into a 60 month case, unless they can pay all creditors in full in less time.

Some changes are "better", such as the changes that reduce the number of repeat or "serial" filings by requiring that the Debtor request either an extension of the Automatic Stay or an imposition of the same. The difficulty in imposing the Stay has truly reduced the number of serial filers.

Some changes, however, are not for the better. Some new processes brought about by these changes have increased the overall costs of bankruptcy. The overall costs of a bankruptcy have been driven up by the creation of a process that is much more administratively burdensome and inefficient.

The other major "noticeable difference" since the passage of BAPCPA is an increase in litigation over various issues. Because of all the new terms and requirements of BAPCPA, a system that otherwise ran smoothly is now chaotic and a morass of indecision. Thus, the system is now slower and more inefficient overall.

CASE STUDY # 5: BRIAN SMALL

The key to success in your bankruptcy case is to become organized and become disciplined in how to handle your financial affairs.

The usual reason people resort to filing bankruptcy is generally related to poor financial judgment, i.e. buying a $40,000 car when a $10,000 car would be sufficient or buying a $400,000 house when a $200,000 house would be just as fine. People have to start living within their means. Just because a lender will grant you credit does not mean that you have to accept it, nor does it mean that you can afford it. Obviously, by the time someone considers bankruptcy due to poor financial decision making, it is too late to undo the damage. What the bankruptcy process does offer is a fresh start, which should include good, solid financial counseling.

The term "successful bankruptcy case" means different things to different people. In my opinion, a "successful" case is one that concludes with the debtor able to withstand the financial pressures of society and that allows the debtor to make a positive contribution to the economy in the future. In order to do that, they must become organized, disciplined, and must learn to avoid the financial pitfalls that forced them into bankruptcy in the first place.

Multiple cases in a Chapter 13 are filed generally for three reasons:

1. The debtor was unable to perform the terms of their repayment plan, i.e. make their Chapter 13 payments, as required in the previous case, and debtor is making a last ditch attempt to save a home, car, and/or other assets.

2. Debtor's prior counsel was incompetent and as such the debtor suffered because of it.

3. Debtor has had a significant change in financial circumstances which now affords them the opportunity to present a successful case, whereas previous issues caused failure, such as loss of income or medical issues that have since resolved.

Most of our judges will generally give a debtor a "second" chance, by

CASE STUDY # 5: BRIAN SMALL

agreeing to extend the automatic stay based on a change in circumstances; however, they are reluctant to impose the automatic stay for a third bankruptcy filed within 12 months after two previous cases have been dismissed.

When an individual is seeking to file a second time, my firm does an in-depth analysis of why they need, or think they need, to file again. I look to make sure that the help we provide is a cure to the entire situation, not just a band-aid on a gaping wound. I advise the client of the seriousness of a second filing. I explain to them that while legally incorrect, the practical fact is this is the last bite of the apple. I tell them that this case must be perfect; that they must do everything they are required to do without fail. The consequences of failure will likely lead to the loss of their home or car. When consulted by a party seeking to file a third or fourth case, I advise the party to seek the advice of another attorney as it is my general policy not to take such cases. I have not filed a third or fourth case for anyone in the past seven years.

The most common mistakes I see debtors make while in bankruptcy are as follows:

1. Failure to communicate with their attorney.

2. Failure to comply with the terms of their Chapter 13 plan.

3. Failure to disclose all of their assets and liabilities.

The most common mistakes I see debtors make when they are discharged from bankruptcy are as follows:

1. Failure to correct the behavior or make different financial choices than those decisions that put them into bankruptcy in the first place, including:

    a.   Incurring new debt, i.e. car, house etc., and/or

    b.   Living beyond their means

2.   Failing to save money for a rainy day, for example a job loss, loss of

CASE STUDY # 5: BRIAN SMALL

overtime or medical issues. Most people are no more than two paychecks away from having to file bankruptcy. Most financial experts recommend that you have a minimum of eight months income saved in a liquid bank account.

The advice I give my clients after discharge is to live within your means, save 15% of your net take home pay each week into a savings/money market account, and pay cash for everything.

The fact is most clients I see generally speaking, are not embarrassed to file bankruptcy. Most people do not worry about the "stigma" of bankruptcy anymore.

They are more interested in what I can do to help them re-establish credit in the future. Of those who are embarrassed, I point out to them that the filing of the bankruptcy provides them with a fresh start and as such we are closing the "old book" and starting to write a "new book" for them. I tell them that rather than dwell on the dismal past, they need to look forward to their bright future.

There are two types of debtors, first are the people who hang on your every word, do everything you tell them to do, and respond to every communication you send them. These are the people you will never see in bankruptcy again. They will be successful because they had a "life event" that caused them to file bankruptcy or the bankruptcy process itself marked that life event.

The second type of debtor is the "irresponsible" debtor. This type of debtor is using the bankruptcy process as a form of financial planning. This debtor will NEVER have complete success in the bankruptcy world. They may get a discharge, but they will continue to suffer one financial crisis after another. They are much like the alcoholic who is unwilling to admit he/she has a drinking problem. They are unwilling to take financial responsibility for their actions and as a result those individuals will not have a successful bankruptcy as they will likely be a repeat filer when they are again eligible.

Some would argue that the second group would be a less educated individual. I suggest otherwise. I think that the basic trait that links the entire second "irresponsible" group is laziness and a belief that the world owes those

CASE STUDY # 5: BRIAN SMALL

individuals a living, almost as if it is an entitlement. The first group, who takes the matter seriously, is comprised of individuals who are studious, caring, and generally hard working. This group takes nothing for granted. This group has more successful cases. This is because not only do they receive a discharge, but the "problem" is generally cured and they will never be back for another bankruptcy. They accept responsibility for their actions and decisions and accept that they are in control of their lives.

CASE STUDY # 6: JASON CARDASIS

Debtor Attorney
Pleasant Ridge, Michigan (serving the Eastern
District of Michigan)

I have been in the bankruptcy field for fourteen
years, all as a debtor attorney.

I have always found it to be a very bad Idea to represent yourself in bankruptcy. It is a very specialized field of law and therefore needs a qualified BK practitioner. In all my years of practicing, I have seen no successful Chapter 11 or 13 cases and very few Chapter 7 cases.

As it is a very complicated process, even with an attorney, my advise for debtors just filing for bankruptcy is simply to be very prepared and listen to the bankruptcy lawyer.

It is very hard to determine the impact that the BAPCPA reform has had on the bankruptcy community because the law is still new. It has some good aspects, but a lot of bad aspects that if Congress just amended in the Pre-BAPCPA law, would have saved a lot of trouble. If I had three days, I could not comment on the change. The law seems to try to force Debtors to file Chapter 13, but I have seen very few cases under BAPCPA where a Chapter 7 would not qualify under the old law. Therefore, I think the new law's intent falls short. But it did give a great benefit to auto finance companies and mortgage companies in the "910" claims (your vehicle must be 910 days or over to be able to be crammed-or paying the secured level only at the value

CASE STUDY # 6: JASON CARDASIS

of the car) and relief aspects under §362. It makes other aspects of Chapter 13 very confusing.

When Debtors file multiple cases, it becomes quite evident if they are abusing the system or need help and prior cases failed due to circumstances beyond their control. How a judge handles this situation depends on the scenario. A good judge will look at each case in an individual light. Not to follow this precept, will result in bad law and determinations. For people considering filing for a second time or third or even more times, at least in a Chapter 13 scenario, they must have a change in circumstance financially to fund a plan and justify the extension of the automatic stay.

One of the most common mistakes I see debtors make is to assume they know the law. They hire lawyers to help, so they need to ask questions and listen!! One of the most common mistakes I see debtors make after they receive their discharge is to run up credit card debt or purchase secured items when their income will not support the purchase.

Once your discharge is issued, it is time to follow the "George Costanza" rule: "Do the exact opposite" of what put them into bankruptcy. On a serious note, it depends on the situation. If a Debtor was living fine, lost a job, incurred medical bills and could not afford everyday, then this type of person does not have a characteristic to spend frivolously. If a Debtor seeks help due to their tendency to spend, then they need to change their style of living, and only buy what they can afford--"pay cash." If they can not afford it without financing, then they should not purchase it. This is a general rule, not the end all meet all.

I have clients that are embarrassed from time to time, but I tell them that they are not alone. Bankruptcy is in place to help people, not to cause embarrassment. Where I practice, in Michigan, bankruptcy is very high; thus most of our clients know someone who filed. It is relief that is justified.

After practicing this long, the debtors cases who succeed are the debtors who are prepared and listen to what I inform them of to succeed. Debtors have to understand that we have seen successful cases; we know what the court, trustees and the creditors want. Therefore, if a Debtor is serious, they

CASE STUDY # 6: JASON CARDASIS

will heed our recommendations and follow them. The most prepared side always wins.

CASE STUDY # 7: MARIA GOTSIS

Former debtor attorney
Current Attorney Administrator
Office of the Chapter 13 Trustee-Krispen S.
Carroll
Detroit, Michigan

I have been in the bankruptcy community since November 2003, holding a few different positions at different areas of the community. I was a law clerk before becoming a debtor attorney at one law firm before moving to another law firm in August 2005. I then became a staff attorney at the Office of the Chapter 13 Trustee—Krispen S. Carroll in August 2006.

It is not advisable for a prospective debtor to file their own Chapter 13 bankruptcy. Although the prospective debtor is legally able to file on their own bankruptcy; it is not a good idea. To borrow a phrase from a former employer, Brian Small (See Case Study #5), when asked if a debtor should file on his or her own, Mr. Small said "It is legal to perform surgery on yourself too, although not advisable." The bankruptcy process, particularly the Chapter 13 process is a complicated one. Failure to comply with the code and local bankruptcy rules can result in the dismissal of the case. A potential debtor has more to lose than just the filing fee if they err in the process of filing their own pro se case. I have seen less than a handful of these cases succeed.

Among other things in a Chapter 13 case, BAPCPA created 60 month commitment periods for above median income debtors. The credit counseling agencies would believe it is better, but it really depends on the district as to if there are noticeable differences between pre- and post-BAPCPA.

In order to have a successful bankruptcy case, it is important that the debtor

CASE STUDY # 7: MARIA GOTSIS

make all of his or her bankruptcy payments. Make sure the plan payment increases upon mortgage escrow changes and that the plan is completing timely. Fulfill the requirements of the plan (including remitting income tax refund obligations if required) and you case will more than likely succeed.

There are a lot of reasons why a debtor may file multiple bankruptcies. Most often, there was a change in financial circumstances (such as the debtor losing his or her job) or the debtor failed to comply with the requirements of the plan. When ruling on multiple cases the judge has an expectation that the debtor understands what is required of them. You need to make all of your payments, provide full disclosure of assets and income, etc.

As a debtor attorney, I did not recommend a second filing. I do not believe I had EVER recommended a third or fourth filing. For many debtors who file subsequent bankruptcies in a short period of time, they have not made a mortgage payment in over a year and the arrearages are astronomical. The debtor would have a very difficult time trying to save their home at that point. Unfortunately, it is very difficult for some people to realize when their home becomes a financial noose around their neck. Their home may just be too expensive for them to keep. In some cases, it may be best to surrender the home and find a reasonable apartment or home to rent. Once the person has saved enough money to purchase a home with a fixed mortgage rate they can afford, then they should do so.

Some of the most common mistakes I have seen debtors make is not taking their bankruptcy seriously enough. For most debtors, this is their last chance to turn things around to keep their home. The mistakes I see recently discharged debtors make is not starting to pay their mortgage payments on their own after the conclusion of the bankruptcy. Other causes are immediately beginning to use credit cards and living beyond their means. To stay out of bankruptcy again in the future, try the following:

- Create an emergency savings account in case you are laid off work or fired. Ideally this would be enough to cover 6-9 months of household expenses.

- Spend less than you earn and live within your means (you are not your belongings)

CASE STUDY # 7: MARIA GOTSIS

- DO NOT USE CREDIT CARDS! Much like the Saturday Night Live skit—if you cannot afford it, do not buy it).

As a debtor attorney I did not find too many embarrassed by having to file for bankruptcy. There were few who would cry during the initial consultation and say they were very embarrassed, but for the most part, people realized this is something the law has made available to them and they wanted to make full use of it.

Debtors who educate themselves about the bankruptcy process and don't make excuses about everything are the ones most likely to receive a discharge and not file bankruptcy again.

CASE STUDY # 8: JASON RAUBENOLT

Senior Mortgage Consultant
Taylor, Michigan

I would not recommend bankruptcy for consumers struggling with debt as the first solution or the only option. I would only suggest filing bankruptcy if all other options have failed for the consumer. Bankruptcy should be used as a last resort.

One of the first steps I would take to try to explore other options would be to prepare a budget. If you are able to identify a break even point for your income and debts, you are less likely to overspend on non-necessity items.

Consider downsizing some of your higher monthly debt. This usually holds true to your mortgage and car notes. Rule of thumb, if you are spending more than 40% of your income on your home loan, you are more than likely in a home that you can not afford and may need to look to more affordable housing. The same model applies to your car note. Maybe this is not the best time to be making payments on a Mercedes when you could be paying off a used model. The recommendations will enable you to put more money to your outstanding creditors.

CASE STUDY # 8: JASON RAUBENOLT

"Cut up your credit cards." This is one that we have all heard a million times; however, cutting up your credit cards can be very affective. Under no circumstances should you be using a credit card (even the emergency card). When you are having financial difficulties your view on what constitutes an emergency could change drastically. Eliminating the temptation is the most realistic way to avoid a relapse.

The biggest problem these days that are putting people into bankruptcy is the consumers' inability to separate need from want. I need shelter; I do not need a 3,000 sq. ft. home with a theatre room!

In today's society we are conditioned to in a sense "keep up with the Jones'." Why wait to save up for a big ticket item when we can charge it today and worry about it later. We are all guilty of this. One purchase leads into several, until we have painted ourselves into a corner. Generations before us were conditioned to save, and put money aside for high ticket items. We could definitely learn form our elders.

Medical bills and illness are also one of the main components to filing bankruptcy which is the most widely overlooked component. In my experience, a great deal of bankruptcy cases has some sort of medical bill tied into them. A single unpaid trip to the emergency room or surgery could leave you with little to no options as far as repayment is concerned. It does not take long for a medical bill to turn into a collection if it is not handled in a timely manner. A sudden illness and an unpaid medical leave can also put you behind the "eight ball." This is where a savings account becomes very important.

My advice to debtors who have recently been discharged from a bankruptcy would be to make sure they are not repeating the same mistakes that led to the bankruptcy. Allow your credit to repair itself over time. Do not try and force the process, you will only prolong the process.

Opening a savings or checking account to cover emergency needs as well as establishing a much needed savings, this will give you breathing room for accidentals.

CASE STUDY # 8: JASON RAUBENOLT

Be sure to check your credit report for errors. You are able to access your credit report once a year at no cost through Equifax, Experian or Transunion. Be sure to review the information thoroughly. Make sure that the debts that were paid off in the bankruptcy as well as the reestablished credit are reporting properly.

There are several things people can do in there daily lives to save money and cut costs. Once again, distinguish between needs and wants. You will be pleasantly surprised on the savings you will see from doing this. Try things out before you buy them and be willing to shop around. Most consumers spend a great deal of money on "toys." Let us take a motorcycle for example. Yes, I have always wanted to ride one but does it make sense? Do I want to pay $200 a month for something that I may only use a few times a year in my area of the country? Try renting or leasing first to make sure it is a sound investment for you. Shop around for the best deal on insurance. More times than not we are going with the first quote we are given and are not properly shopping around.

Cutting costs on your food bill is also a great way to save money. Try and consider store brands or generics. If you know you are going to use items in larger quantities buy in bulk or stock up on sale items. Try eating out one less time a week and put that money into your savings. An extra $20 a week would put almost $1,000 in your account over a year.

I would advise people to make sure they are learning from their mistakes and that they are making an effort to rebuild their credit. Use your bankruptcy as a wake-up call. If medical bills were your downfall, try and make sure you are covering yourself with insurance, cut other spending to allow for this.

If you lost your job and filed bankruptcy because of a lack of savings, make your savings account your top priority. Have $50 from each paycheck deducted and deposited directly into a savings account. Limit the access to the account to deter you from withdrawing your savings. If your problem was overspending, make the necessary changes needed. Do not take away all of your spending ability. Allow yourself the opportunity to buy the "want" items as opposed to just the needs.

CASE STUDY # 8: JASON RAUBENOLT

Reestablishing credit after a bankruptcy is very important. Getting an unsecured credit card will most likely be out of the question. Go to your local bank and apply for a secured credit card. Installment loans such as your car, mortgage or school loans can also help establish your credit. Besides paying your bills on time, paying down existing debt also helps repair your credit. In a perfect world you will want three open and active trade lines on your credit report. Timely payments on the accounts are a must. If you have established new credit make sure you are not borrowing more than 30% of the limit. Be sure to pay off the balances every month, this will help your credit a great deal.

I have been able to obtain a loan for clients currently in and recently discharged from the bankruptcy. Typically lenders like to see the consumers bankruptcy discharged for at least 24 months. An elapsed period of less than two years may be acceptable if the borrower can show extenuating circumstances beyond their control, and has since exhibited a documented ability to manage their financial affairs in a responsible manner. If still in the bankruptcy, the debtor must also have permission from the court for the lender to enter into the transaction.

CASE STUDY # 9: ALANNA ERVING

Financial Administrator
Office of the Chapter 13 Trustee-Krispen S. Carroll
Detroit, Michigan

I have been working at the bankruptcy trustee's office for five years in various roles.

I do not feel it is wise for a debtor to represent themselves in bankruptcy because the laws are extensive and confusing. Most attorneys, who do not specialize in bankruptcy, are sometimes unable to provide their clients with the type of representation they deserve.

CLASSIFIED CASE STUDIES
directly from the experts

CASE STUDY # 9: ALANNA ERVING

So, I think an average everyday person with little to no legal background and no bankruptcy experience will have a tough time getting a case confirmed and then seeing it through to the end. In most instances, pro se cases are dismissed before their first meeting.

I would not suggest bankruptcy as a first option. A person considering bankruptcy needs to change their spending habits by cutting back or making and sticking to a budget. A discharge in a bankruptcy case will not mean a thing if saving and cutting back do not become a lifestyle. Patterns are not changed to prevent people from returning to credit cards using them to make ends meet or buying those expensive items they could not afford in the first place. A person considering bankruptcy should exhaust all other options first. Such as credit counseling, trying to make arrangements with creditors themselves, or possibly surrendering those assets that put them in this position in the first place.

Most people do not want to give up their big houses or big cars, but sometimes that is what is necessary to save money and get out of debt. If possible take a second, part-time job to begin whittling away at debt. By having extra income, people are able to contribute more than the minimum due on loans and retire high interest loans early.

One of the biggest problems putting people in bankruptcy these days is the economy, "teaser" rate mortgages, and negligent creditors with lapse credit issuing policies. The economy in the US is at its worst in years and debtors are not seeing any relief except bankruptcy. In some cases this is a lifesaver in others it could be a nightmare. Creditors, who qualify unworthy borrowers, are not doing the economy or their bottom lines any favors. Eventually adjustable rates will kick in and the loans that began with interest only payments will begin to include principal. These types of mortgages are fine in the beginning, but when the payment balloons to its normal monthly payment most borrowers cannot afford them. The only way to have good credit is to establish, it or in the case of bankruptcy, re-establish it. I would say after your discharge to start off slowly with one credit card. Only charge what can be paid off in a month and never carry that card. Having it handy leads to excess, unnecessary purchases. If you really want something, save the cash for it or try putting it in layaway so you can pay on it in installments.

CASE STUDY # 9: ALANNA ERVING

There are a few simple things people can do to save money. Whenever you are paid you should try to set a weekly allowance aside for yourself and make purchases with that cash. Constantly paying by debit does not allow a daily record of how much is being spent. If you can see the cash going out and keep a balance; then you make less impulse purchases say at the last minute while waiting in line. Bring lunch to work. Buy a thermos for coffee or tea to avoid going to pricey coffeehouses. For entertainment, try finding free festivals, concerts, or art exhibits in your town.

The advice I have for people recently discharged from bankruptcy is to stop living beyond your means.

CASE STUDY # 10: ANDREA RUIZ

Paralegal in Creditor Work
Stovash, Case & Tingley, P.A.

I have been in the bankruptcy for five years and have held various jobs in the field.

I feel an individual can represent themselves in a bankruptcy case only if it is a very simple Chapter 7 case, but for the more complex bankruptcy, Chapter 13, it is in the debtor's best interest to be represented by an attorney. I have actually seen only a handful of Chapter 7 cases filed as Pro Se succeed and these were cases with no assets and the case was filed for only for unsecured debt.

In order to make your bankruptcy a success make sure all of your debt is listed and have a plan on how to handle all future finances. When I have seen multiple cases filed by the same individual over a short period of time I have found it usually relates to unnecessary spending habits, there are many people living beyond their means.

Debtors make some common mistakes while in bankruptcy and after their

CASE STUDY # 10: ANDREA RUIZ

discharge. While in their case, they may not include all of their debts in their petition. The mistakes I see after discharge are debtors seeking to rebuild their credit scores by obtaining high interest credit cards and running up another debt. The interest rates are high, limits are low and they may end up with multiple cards. For those debtors just emerging out of bankruptcy I would advise them to seek a financial consultant who can help establish a budget for all of their living expenses.

Working in the creditor area of bankruptcy, I know that there are some ways to minimize the objections a creditor may have. I look to see that my client's debt has been properly identified and any and all re-affirmation of said debt.

Sometimes creditors would rather have a debtor file a bankruptcy than go down other avenues. One of these times could be during a foreclosure matter when the debtor can afford the payments, but they just happened to hit a financial hardship (loss of income, family illness, etc.). The bank does not want a house that the debtor can afford; they just need some time to reestablish their finances.

CASE STUDY # 11: KRISPEN CARROLL

Chapter 13 Bankruptcy Trustee
Detroit, Michigan

I have spent all of my 14 years of law in bankruptcy related practice. I spent my first three years at a firm representing commercial creditors in Chapters 7, 11 and 13 and acting as counsel for Chapter 7 Trustees. I spent the next three years as staff attorney for David Ruskin, Chapter 13 Trustee. I received my own appointment as Chapter 13 Trustee in April of 2000.

I always advise debtors to hire legal counsel. You wouldn't try to remove your own appendix or drill your own tooth. Why try to handle your own legal proceedings? With the passage the bankruptcy amendments in 2005 and

CASE STUDY # 11: KRISPEN CARROLL

the requirements to file and complete a means test, the forms are now significantly more complicated than was previously so. Even a well educated debtor would have little knowledge of the requirements of the bankruptcy code and the required disclosures. While a Chapter 7 bankruptcy may be said to be easier to file yourself, the filing of a Chapter 7 petition is riskier from the sense that it cannot be voluntarily dismissed by the debtor. If the filing results in a determination by the trustee that there are assets to be administered, the debtor's options are limited.

I have no idea about the success rate of Chapter 7 cases without counsel. In the 11 years I have been trustee or trustee counsel, I have seen less than 10 pro se cases confirmed. I am not aware of any pro se cases in my office that have completed the case and received a discharge. (This does not include cases where the debtor originally had counsel that withdrew before the completion of the case. I have probably had 3 or 4 cases that have completed where debtor's counsel had withdrawn or was deceased.)

My experience with BAPCPA in southeast Michigan has been that, on the whole, it has produced a decrease overall in bankruptcy filings. This is primarily due to the limitations on filings in Chapter 13s and the limitations on the ability of the debtor to obtain an automatic stay where the debtor had a previous bankruptcy filing. It has complicated the process for confirmation of a Chapter 13 case with little noticeable advantages for creditors or others involved in the process. My overall caseload continues to drop since the implementation of the legislation in October of 2005.

This new law has also come about during the same time that adjustable rate mortgages have become the norm for Chapter 13 debtors. While the Means Test often requires greater dividends from debtors to unsecured creditors, they are also faced with fluctuating interest rates of their mortgage which make these dividends unattainable.

Debtor's need to think about belt-tightening and careful budgeting when putting together their schedules, but they also need to be realistic. Debtors often underestimate their basic expenses such as food, utilities, clothing, medical, etc. The occurrence of unrealistically low budgets is far higher than the occurrence of inflated budgets. Debtors whose cases confirm

CASE STUDY # 11: KRISPEN CARROLL

with larger budgets and shorter plan lengths have a far greater chance of completion and discharge. There is simply more room for adjustment when changes occur.

My assumption when I see a debtor who has multiple filings over a short period of time is either that the debtor is unrealistic about their abilities to make the necessary payments to save their home or the debtor is attempting to "play" the system (less likely after BAPCPA). It's been my experience that bankruptcy judges make similar assumptions about debtors with multiple filings. They set a higher threshold for such filers and give considerably less credence to the arguments of debtors with prior filings.

Debtors assume that because no collection agency is calling them when they miss a few payments to the Trustee, that no real harm has occurred. Unlike outside of bankruptcy, a considerable delinquency has occurred before a motion is filed by a creditor or the trustee. By the time a debtor gets serious about addressing a problem with their bankruptcy, the delinquency may be beyond the debtor's ability to cure. This is often the case with tax refunds which can be large amounts. A debtor, who uses a tax refund for unapproved expenses, may have difficulty paying back those amounts during the plan term.

Debtors often fail to begin making continuing mortgage payments when directed by the trustee at the conclusion of the case. A debtor who fails to timely restart direct payments can accrue a delinquency of their mortgage before their discharge is even entered. Mortgage companies may also take advantage of the debtor by failing to discharge all required debts at the end of the plan. This is a difficult position for a debtor whose bankruptcy attorney has typically closed their file and may not be willing to assist the debtor in enforcing the discharge.

Debtors should avoid having multiple credit card accounts. While reestablishing credit with a single credit account may be beneficial, only amounts that can be paid in full at the end of the month should be charged on the card. Don't use equity in your home or loans against your 401k to pay off unsecured debts such as credit cards. If you should find yourself needing

CASE STUDY # 11: KRISPEN CARROLL

bankruptcy relief in the future, these assets are largely out of reach of your creditors. They also are your last safety net. Once they are gone your financial stability becomes extremely fragile.

Bibliography

Aranda, Natalie, "The Myths and Facts about Personal Bankruptcy," **<http://ezinearticles.com/?The-Myths-and-Facts-about-Personal-Bankruptcy&id=466193>**, accessed on March 15, 2008.

Bankruptcy Code and Rules, 2008 ed., Thomson/West, 2008.

"Bankruptcy History," **http://www.bankruptcylawinformation.com/index.cfm?event=dspHistory**, accessed on March 15, 2008.

"BAPCPA: The Bankruptcy Abuse Prevention and Consumer Protection Act," **http://www.jaxlawcenter.com/lawyer-attorney-1214992.html**, accessed on March 14, 2008.

Elias, Stephen, *The New Bankruptcy: Will It Work for You?*, 2d ed., Delta Printing Solutions, Inc., Berkley, Calif., 2007.

Elias, Stephen, et al., *Chapter 7 Bankruptcy*, 14th ed., Delta Printing Solutions, Inc., Berkley, Calif., 2007

Elias, Stephen and Leonard, Robin, *Chapter 13 Bankruptcy: Repay Your Debts*, 8th ed., Delta Printing Solutions, Inc., Berkley, Calif., 2006.

Gallop.com, "Public Shows Little Love for Bush, Congress," March 14, 2008, **http://www.gallup.com/poll/104989/Public-Shows-Little-Love-Bush-Congress.aspx**, accessed on March 16, 2008.

Great Quotes, **http://www.great-quotes.com**, accessed on February 15, 2008.

Hartford and Cecil's Community Credit Union, "Bankruptcy Myth vs. Facts," **http://www.apgfcu.com/other/bankruptcy.asp**, accessed on March 15, 2008.

"How to Use the Foreclosure Redemption Period," **http://www.foreclosurefish.com/blog/index.php?id=216**, accessed on March 15, 2008.

Kulla, Bridget, "Frugal Food: Six Ways to Save Money on Groceries," **http://www.fastweb.com/fastweb/resources/articles/index/110303?id=**, accessed on March 27, 2008.

Leonard, Robin and Lamb, John, *Solve Your Money Troubles*, 11th ed., Delta Printing Solutions, Inc., Berkley, Calif., 2007.

"Means Test Changes May Help Some Consumers, Hurt Others," **http://blogs.nolo.com/bankruptcy/2007/12/21/means-test-changes-may-help-some-consumers-hurt-others-in-2008**, accessed on March 5, 2008.

Meyer, Cathy, "Ask.com: Divorce Support, How Much Should I Expect my Divorce to Cost?," **http://divorcesupport. about.com/od/canyouaffordtodivorce/f/divorce_cost. htm**, accessed on February 15, 2008.

"Myths on Bankruptcy: Taking Down the Myths Surrounding Bankruptcy," **http://bankruptcy-aid. com/wordpress/2005/11/24/myths-on-bankruptcy-exposed**, accessed on March 15, 2008.

"The New Bankruptcy Law," **http://bankruptcy.findlaw. com/new-bankruptcy-law/new-bankruptcy-law-basics/ big-changes.html**, accessed on February 12, 2008.

Palms, Peggy, *The Bankruptcy Solution: How to Eliminate Debt and Rebuild Your Life*, Adams Media, Avon, Mass., 2003.

"10 Questions Before Getting A Secured Credit Card," **http://www.bankrate.com/brm/news/cc/19990823. asp**, accessed on April 3, 2008.

U.S. Trustee Program, **http://www.usdoj.gov/ust/index. htm**, accessed on February 8, 2008.

Wikipedia, "Bankruptcy," **http://en.wikipedia.org/wiki/ Bankruptcy**, accessed on March 15, 2008.

Wikipedia, "St. Johns County, Florida," **http:// en.wikipedia.org/wiki/St._Johns_County,_Florida**, accessed on February 20, 2008.

Yip, Pamela, "Rebuild Your Credit After Bankruptcy," *The Orlando Sentinel*, March 9, 2008, p. G1, G5

Acknowledgements

To my wife, Tamara: Thank you for dreaming my dream for me and always being understanding of the silliness of being married to me.

To my baby girl, Kelsey: I never felt emptier and sadder than that month we were apart. I missed you more than you will ever know. That song on the dumb AT&T Wireless commercial will always remind me of you whenever we are apart in the future.

"Sweet pea

Apple of my eye

Don't know when and I don't know why

You're the only reason I keep on coming home"

-"*Sweet Pea*" by Amos Lee

To my mom: Who, by introducing me to the world of bankruptcy, paved the way for my very first book.

To my ex-colleagues and friends Alanna, Janet, Jeremiah, Kristen and Venita: Thanks for making life at the trustee's office a blast. I'll always look back fondly on our C.A. lunches, the St. Louis trip, the Happy Tree Friends and that pesky squirrel problem we had. Long live the Dork Squad!

About the Author

Matt Pelc worked in the trenches of the bankruptcy world while employed at one of the Chapter 13 trustee's offices in Detroit, Michigan for nearly six years. He held a few posts at Trustee Krispen S. Carroll's Office and had many experiences dealing with Chapter 13 debtors, including reviewing their cases and holding their 341 Meetings.

Matt followed his dream of writing to Florida and left the trustee's office in early 2008. He now works as a freelance writer in Davenport, Florida and resides with his wife, Tamara, and their two-year-old daughter, Kelsey.

Besides writing, Matt's passions include being a long-suffering Detroit Lion fan and following the Detroit Tigers and other Michigan-based sports teams. His interests are trains, history, and watching his young daughter grow and get ever smarter each day.

Peruse Matt's writings at **pelcprofessionalwriting.com**, and feel free to contact him at **matt@pelcprofessional-writing.com**.